SECRET AGENT MAN

Essays

Margot Singer

©2025 by Margot Singer
All rights reserved

Cover Design: Catherine Charbonneau
Interior Design: Michelle Caraccia

Published 2025 by Barrow Street, Inc.
(501) (c) (3) corporation. All contributions are tax deductible.
Distributed by:
    Barrow Street Books
    c/o University of Rhode Island
    English Department, Swan 114
    60 Upper College Road
    Kingston, RI 02881

Barrow Street Books are distributed by Itasca Books Distribution &
Fulfillment, 210 Edge Place, Minneapolis MN, 55418, itascabooks.com.
Telephone (844) 488-4477; amazon.com; Ingram Periodicals Inc., 1240
Heil Quaker Blvd, PO Box 7000, La Vergne, TN 37086-700 (615) 213-
3574; and Armadillo & Co., 7310 S. La Cienega Blvd, Inglewood, CA
90302, (310) 693-6061.

Special thanks to the University of Rhode Island English Department
and especially the PhD Program in English, 60 Upper College Road,
Swan 114, Kingston, RI 02881, (401) 874-5931, which provides valuable
in-kind support, including graduate and undergraduate interns.

First Edition

Library of Congress Control Number: 2025933038

ISBN: 978-1-962131-07-0

SECRET AGENT MAN

Essays

Margot Singer

Barrow Street Press
New York City

CONTENTS

SECRET AGENT MAN	1
GOD'S EYE	21
THE POWER SUIT	43
CALL IT RAPE	49
GHOST VARIATIONS	67
THE BRAHMIC EGG	89
AFTERIMAGE	97
A NATURAL HISTORY OF SMALL-TOWN OHIO	111
COUNTERCLOCKWISE	123
AUTHOR'S NOTE	143
ABOUT THE AUTHOR	147

for my father

SECRET AGENT MAN

1.

Spies dress in black and carry attaché cases. They may disguise themselves as diplomats, business executives, exotic dancers, academics, scientists, consultants, epileptics, holy men.

Spies possess their own geometry. They have dimension, volume, angles, planes: a surface and an underneath.

Spies listen through keyholes. They squint through one eye.

Spies collect passports, languages, bugs, maps, lovers, offshore bank accounts, gadgets, covers, ciphers, names.

A spy is a trick of perspective. If a spy turns sideways, he may disappear.

Spies used to send dispatches from clandestine thirty-two-pound radio transmitters, but not anymore.

Spies may be sleepers, dangles, walk-ins, plants, special agents, station chiefs, or moles. They may be single or double. They may be blown or burned.

Spies never go to AA meetings. Spies don't talk about the past.

Spies disappear into the background. They wear button-up shirts and reading glasses, just like all your father's friends.

You can poke your finger through a spy. He will scatter like ash.

2.

My father had the kind of face people thought they'd seen somewhere before. My high school friends thought he looked like Ricardo Montalban on *Fantasy Island*. A boyfriend thought he looked like George H. W. Bush. When, in his twenties, he wore a thin mustache, people said he looked

1

like Clark Gable. Once I came across his double in a glossy magazine. I flipped a page and did a double take. There he was, with a drink in one hand (it was an advertisement for Pernod), a cigarette in the other, wearing a black turtleneck and a houndstooth blazer, his legs crossed jauntily. I cut the picture out and sent it to him. He laughed and pinned it up on the corkboard over his desk at home, where it still hangs, curling at the edges and pocked with push-pin holes, next to a drawing of a sailboat I made when I was nine or ten, that says "I love you, Daddy" inside a crayoned heart.

3.

My father was born in Czechoslovakia but immigrated with his family to Palestine in 1940, when he was nine. He spoke English with an accent as a result: a mixture of German and Czech and Israeli with a vaguely British lilt. When I was growing up, he wore Brioni suits, smoked three packs of Larks a day, and drove a Porsche. He traveled a good deal on business, to places like New York and Tel Aviv, Tokyo and Cairo, Dhaka and Dubai. Exotic visitors passed through our home: a diplomat from Dahomey, an Egyptian textile magnate, the Indian musician Bismillah Khan and his troupe (who gave a concert by our swimming pool), a Japanese executive, a Polish painter, and a steady stream of Israeli expats like himself. In the preppy Boston suburb where I grew up, he wasn't like anybody else's dad.

Who was he? Not really American, no longer Czech or European, not even Israeli, exactly, although that is usually what I said if someone asked. He tended to be evasive on this point. He told no childhood stories; he seemed to have little interest in the past. We teased him for saying "birzday" instead of "birthday" and mixing up the words "fingers" and "toes," but English was the only language we spoke at home, the language he used with his German-speaking parents and his Hebrew-speaking relatives and friends.

My mother liked to tell a story about the time a business associate came to dinner who spoke only French, a language my father had never learned. My mother, who had studied French in high school, did her best, but the conversation, understandably, was strained. She was in the kitchen, she said, when a roar of laughter erupted from the dining room. *Exactement!* she heard the Frenchman exclaim. *Tu me comprends parfaitement!* I will never know, my mother said, what your father said to that man and whether he actually understood anything at all.

4.

It is said that espionage is the world's second-oldest profession. The fourth book of Moses tells how two of Joshua's spies were saved by the prostitute Rahab, who hid them on her roof, helping to bring the walls of Jericho tumbling down. The Egyptian pharaoh Thutmose III smuggled spies in flour sacks into the besieged city of Jaffa in 1468 BCE. Warring princes in twelfth-century Japan used ninja as spies and silent assassins; the word "ninja" comes from the Japanese for "to make yourself invisible." Medieval troubadours spied by eavesdropping as they entertained noblemen in their castles. Since Canaanite times, traders and businessmen have kept their eyes and ears open on their travels and reported back on what they observed.

5.

From time to time, when I was little, my father brought things home from work. Once he gave me a blue-and-white-striped denim cap, and because he'd told me he was an engineer, I pictured him leaning out the window of a chuffing train, waving a sooty hand, like an illustration in a children's book. He brought home ashtrays and towels swiped from luxury hotels; he returned from business trips with embroidered textiles, Nigerian sculptures, Japanese kimonos, a fur-covered Ethiopian drum. He gave me a paper dress printed with bright red and yellow flowers, an entire sample line of French skiwear, a mink teddy bear with diamond chips for buttons, and a lamp that you could turn on and off by squeezing a squeaky rubber ball—or, as I discovered to my mother's dismay, by screeching at an extremely loud, high pitch.

These objects were like artifacts uncovered in a dig: fragments imbued with value but whose context wasn't clear. I remember, in particular, the purple carpet in the shape of an enormous footprint that I stared at, frozen in fear, the morning I found it on my bathroom floor, until it slowly lost the aspect of a crater crushed into the tile by an evil giant and reassumed the contours of a fuzzy rug.

6.

My father worked as an independent consultant. He maintained a long-term contract with the Boston-based management consulting firm, Arthur D. Little, and every once in a while, he'd take me with him to work. The firm's offices were in a modern industrial office park with glass-walled sky bridges and echoing stairwells with open metal treads. My father had a narrow, dim, shoebox office with a bookshelf along one wall and a desk against the other. The books on the shelves were about textile engineering and entrepreneurship and innovation, my father's areas of expertise. A few of the spines had Hebrew lettering, which I couldn't read. He'd doodle on a pad of graph paper as he talked on the phone, enclosing words in boxes and underlining or retracing them. He wrote in a mixture of upper- and lower-case letters, loopy and hard to decipher. Sometimes I could make out numbers or a cryptic phrase.

On the days I tagged along, he'd make a few phone calls while I colored or read, and then he'd walk me up and down the corridors to meet his colleagues, men in open-collared shirts with pocket protectors and aviator glasses. I'd stand there, twisting onto the outside of my shoes or picking at my nails, as he bragged about my grades and piano playing to the other men. Then he'd take me to the company cafeteria for lunch. It astonished me that my father ate in a cafeteria so similar to the one we had at school, serving the kind of typically American food we hardly ever ate at home. After lunch, he'd pack his pens and pads of paper back into his briefcase, and we'd drive home again.

My father never seemed to work very hard. In fact, he often proudly proclaimed that he never worked for anyone other than himself and never for more than nine months out of every year. It seemed clear that he made plenty of money anyway. I considered him very successful and important. Of course, I had no clue about what he really did.

7.

Consulting is the perfect cover for a spy. Like spies, consultants handle cases, are taken into confidence, conduct fact-based analysis, possess strong inductive reasoning skills, deliver classified reports. Consultants have access to important people and top secret information. They take care to encrypt their data, shred old files, shield their laptop screens from prying eyes. They never divulge their clients' names, not even to the closest members of their families. They don't discuss their work in places where anyone might overhear. They have plausible reasons for asking probing questions, carrying attaché cases, traveling overseas.

Valerie Plame posed as a private energy consultant for a CIA front company before her cover was breached by a journalist in 2003. The Russian spy Donald Heathfield (a.k.a. Andrei Bezrukov) collected intelligence for the KGB while employed by Global Partners, a Boston-based international consulting and management development firm. During the 1950s and '60s, the famous CIA agent Miles Copeland worked under the cover of the management consulting firm Booz Allen Hamilton in the Middle East.

Few people really understand what consultants do, which helps. I know, because I too worked as a management consultant for many years, although I never traded in any intelligence but my own.

8.

Well into his eighties, my father kept busy advising high-tech start-ups, an Israeli security firm, an outfit seeking to farm barramundi in the Negev. He helped organize a conference aimed at promoting peace by creating call-center jobs in the West Bank. Folders and pads of paper covered in his illegible scribbles were piled on his desk. He could be heard muttering about how he'd been awake all night solving problems in his head.

"What exactly does your father do, again?" my husband asked. Like my mother's cousins, who used to pull my brother and me aside at holiday gatherings and ask in whispers if our father *really* worked for the Mossad, my husband liked to joke that my father had to be a spy. His own father had been a lineman for the electric company. There was nothing mysterious in that.

We entertained ourselves by watching the old British TV spy series from the 1960s, *Danger Man, a.k.a. Secret Agent.* We laughed at the psychedelic title sequence, at superspy John Drake's assortment of hats, the women's miniskirts and bouffant hair, the Eastern Bloc bad guys, the rotary telephones, the clunky gadgets (an enormous video monitor concealed inside a wine cask, a camera disguised as an alarm clock). The political drama of those Cold War days now seemed so tame, what was once hip and thrilling devolved to camp. It made us laugh. It made us feel nostalgic. It was the '60s, the landscape of our childhoods, turned cheesy and remote.

Secret agent man, secret agent man, Johnny Rivers sings as the opening credits roll. *They've given you a number and taken away your name.*

My father's given name was Kurt, but as a teenager in the 1940s he changed it to the less Germanic-sounding Dan. Not Daniel, never Danny, but Dan, after the Biblical tribe, pronounced the Hebrew way (to rhyme with "Khan"). My uncle took the name of another tribe, Benjamin, though everybody called him "Bambi." Only my grandparents called him Felix, *lucky,* the name they'd given him, instead.

Like "Danger Man" John Drake (played by the Irish-American actor Patrick McGoohan, who was about the same age as my dad), my father had dark blue eyes, a square chin, brown hair parted on the right, a Dictaphone, an attaché case, more than one passport, a ready supply of cigarettes, pocket handkerchiefs, and calfskin driving gloves, an evasive manner, an accent, a clean shave. Like John Drake, he traveled around the world for work. And like John Drake—to the best of my knowledge, at least—he enjoyed good food and wine, abstained from frivolous love affairs, and did not carry a gun.

9.

My best friend Lisa and I played *Mission Impossible* in second grade. We stood solemnly in front of her transistor radio, pretending it was a reel-to-reel tape player, and intoned, *Good morning, Mr. Phelps,* and *Your mission, Jim, should you decide to accept it,* and *This tape will self-destruct in five seconds,* and *Good luck, Jim,* just like on TV.

I don't recall the plotlines of any of the episodes we made up, though I do remember the time we got shut in the squash court located off the kitchen of the cottage Lisa's parents rented on an equestrian estate. We were taking turns riding our spy mobile (her younger sister's tricycle) in circles around the court. The door leading back into the kitchen was at least a foot thick and heavy as a tree trunk, so when we couldn't get it open, no one heard us pounding and yelling for quite a while. I remember the white glare of the walls and floor, the way the light filtered in from high rectangular windows reinforced with wire, the echo of our voices, the muffled thumping of our fists.

10.

As a child, I was a shameless snoop. I rooted around in the pantry cupboards, my father's desk, my mother's purse, jacket pockets, bureau drawers, closet shelves. I found a hot-pink paperback copy of Xaviera Hollander's *The Happy Hooker* buried among my mother's socks, along with *Everything You Ever Wanted to Know About Sex* *But Were Afraid to Ask.* I found a packet of cigarette papers and a rolling device inside a hidden compartment in my father's dresser. At the back of a bathroom shelf, I found two pornographic pamphlets (disappointingly, with German text), one depicting a scrawny man having sex with two women at once, the other a group of topless lesbians in chains and leather pants. In the bathroom, I found my father's Brylcreem and my mother's diaphragm.

I studied photographs of my parents taken before I was born: in ski clothes in Kitzbühel and at Tuckerman Ravine, at glamorous-looking parties and luxurious-looking resorts. In one picture, my mother has dressed up for a costume party in a yellow minidress and thigh-high boots, my father in paint-covered jeans and a borrowed Hells Angels leather vest. In another, my mom is mugging for the camera in my uncle's Israeli army jacket, holding his rifle, her chin cocked in the air, a mustache penciled on her upper lip.

Spies, of course, run the risk of learning things they'd rather not have known. Once I hid behind the clothes in the back of my parents' closet while they were fighting, and between my mother's sobs and my father's muttered threats, I realized they were arguing about me. Another time, I answered the phone and, instead of hanging up after my mother picked up the extension, I overheard her ordering my birthday present, about which I later had to pretend to be surprised. Not having learned my lesson, in graduate school I peeked in my boyfriend's journal and discovered that he thought I didn't listen well and talked too much about myself. I guess it was good to know these things, although it didn't seem so at the time.

11.

On Parents' Day in seventh grade, my classmate Lynnie passed me a note in Latin class that read: "Does your father

wear a rug?" I had no idea what she meant. She snickered as
she leaned over and whispered the meaning in my ear. My
father sat on my other side, listening with a bored expression
to the teacher's explanation of Latin verb declensions,
twiddling his thumbs. I tried to glance surreptitiously at his
scalp. I couldn't tell if the pale patches between the follicles
of hair were canvas or skin. They looked like skin to me. But
at that moment, I understood why he never put his head
underwater in the pool, why he took baths instead of showers,
why he always wore a hat out in the sun. I thought of my
grandfather and uncle, whose heads were as bald as eggs on
top with just the thinnest fringe of white.

In our family, no one had ever said a word about
my father's hair. And yet, once I knew, it seemed all too
obvious—a blown cover, in plain sight.

12.

My father, at my house for a visit, came up behind me
and leaned over my shoulder to look at my computer screen,
startling me. "What?" I said, annoyed. He often stood a little
too close, riffled through my books and papers, got in my
personal space.

"How do you find out information about somebody
on the internet?" he asked.

"Like what information?" I said.

"Like about me, like where I went to school, things
like that."

It was the early 2000s, and Google was not yet five
years old. I attempted to explain what a search engine was
and how it worked. To illustrate, I typed my name into the
search bar and scrolled through a page or two of hits—a few
relevant, mostly not.

Having quit smoking some years back, my father

carried tins of tiny pill-like mints around in his pocket that rattled as he walked. He took out the mints now and offered me one, then said, "So, you can get any information you want about a person, just like that?"

I explained that what came up depended on what was out there on the web.

"So what's out there on me?" he said.

"How should I know?"

"Put my name in," he said.

And so I did, and he leaned even farther over my shoulder as I scrolled through pages of links to websites featuring people with his name: realtors, music researchers, retired state troopers, used-car salesmen, tennis players, even a few consultants, as well as a surprisingly large number of singer-songwriters named Dan.

My father straightened up, rattling his mints. He said, "Well, it's good to know there's nothing there."

I swiveled around in my chair. "Is there something in particular you're concerned about?"

"Oh, people have asked."

"People? What people? Asked what?"

But he just turned away.

13.

On *Danger Man,* the married agents never tell their wives that they are spies. You'd think the wives would get suspicious when, for example, their husbands make them ditch their belongings at a hotel and race to the airport on a moment's notice, or when armed thugs just happen to be standing in their living room when they come home early from a play, but they never push too hard when their husbands evade their questions or invent a lame excuse. They are just wives, after all.

Sometime in the late 1990s, my father started going to Connecticut on occasional weekends. He said that he was meeting some Saudis there who had a yacht. He offered no further details. My father had served in the early days of the Israeli navy's famous underwater demolition unit, Shayetet (Flotilla) 13, and he liked to sail, unlike the rest of our seasick family. But sailing with a bunch of Saudis? What was up with that?

My mother knew no more than I did. She didn't want to know, she said. Her attitude annoyed me. "What if he's visiting his girlfriend?" I said, just to be obnoxious. "Maybe he's got a whole other family you don't even know about!" I'd come across news stories about this kind of thing.

My mother made a face. "He never tells me *anything*," she said. It was her perpetual complaint.

After 9/11, I grew even more concerned. Dealing with a bunch of rich, yacht-sailing Saudis in Connecticut seemed like an especially bad idea just then.

"Why do you let him get away with this?" I asked my mom.

"We've been married for nearly fifty years," she said, as if that settled it.

I bit my tongue. What did I know? None of it made sense to me.

14.

It was my father who taught me the value of a lie. I was seven the summer he turned forty, and when my mother decided to throw him a surprise party, she let me in on the secret, and I promised not to tell. My father was not pleased about reaching middle age. He sulked and pouted, exhaling clouds of pipe smoke out his nose and swearing at my mother, as he often did, under his breath. He would not celebrate, he declared. He pulled shut the accordion doors that divided his office from the front hall, yelled at us to be quiet, spoke loudly in Hebrew on the phone.

The problem arose the day before the party, when he glimpsed my mother sneaking out the back door to hide the birthday cake in our neighbor's fridge. As soon as she was out of sight, he came up to me and grabbed me by the upper arm. It was June. I remember him in shorts, hairy-chested without a shirt. He wasn't a particularly big man, but he had a way of glaring down his nose and setting his jaw that could be quite severe. And I was little then.

"I want you to tell me," he said, his accent making the words sound scarier than they were. "Is your mother planning a party for me?" He tightened his grip, pulling me close. "Tell me the truth," he warned.

I squirmed. My face went hot. "Oh, no," I lied. "The *neighbors* are having a party. They asked Mommy to keep *their* cake in *our* fridge, because there wasn't any room in theirs."

I remember the rush of exhilaration as the words came out, unpremeditated, tidy as a geometric proof. I'd like to think I looked him in the eye. Of course he believed me. He let go of my arm and the muscles in his jaw relaxed. Thanks to me, the party was a complete success. And when my mother told the story of how I'd saved the day, everyone praised me for my duplicity, including, of course, my dad.

15.

I wanted to talk to my father about all of his mysterious dealings, but I found it hard to start. What questions should I ask? How hard should I press for answers? Would he tell me the truth? It was easier to say nothing. Months slid by, then years. Finally, I asked if I could interview him for an essay I was thinking of writing about him. He readily agreed. In fact, he seemed thrilled.

We sat outside on my porch in Salt Lake City. Across the valley, the mountains shimmered in the summer heat. He told me about how he'd studied textile engineering in Leicester, England, in the 1940s, and how he built a reputation by writing articles about knitting methodology for trade journals in the States. He told me about the consulting projects he'd taken on for the governments of Nigeria, Japan, Egypt, Tunisia, Bangladesh. He told me about the start-up he founded with an Israeli friend who'd invented the remote-controlled fiber-optic catheter, and how, after they sold it, that company went on to become the medical-device giant, Boston Scientific. He described the work he did to help privatize Czech companies after the Velvet Revolution, returning to the Czech Republic for the first time since he'd fled the Nazi occupation fifty years before. He told me about his other ventures, too: a record label in Paris, an art gallery in SoHo. He talked and I took notes. Many of the stories were familiar to me, although some were not, and I learned many new details. He was proud of what he'd done, and I was proud as well. Most of all, I was happy to see the pleasure he took in telling his life story to me.

It occurred to me, as I listened, that maybe he wasn't keeping any big dramatic secret, after all. Maybe, as my mother so often complained, he simply didn't have the words. Or maybe I had never asked. Maybe I had never really listened, either, until then.

16.

Spies like to speak in euphemisms. "Sending a person on vacation" means that they'll be injured; if it's a long vacation, they'll be badly hurt. Sending them to a "better world" means they won't be back. A "blind date" is a meeting between a contact and their controller. A "dead drop" is a way to hand off secret files. "Active measures" are operations to influence other nations' policies. "Dry cleaning" refers to actions taken to avoid surveillance. A "music box" is a transmitter; a "diamond" is a kind of bug. A "cold approach" is an attempt to recruit a foreign national. To set a "honey trap" is to seek intelligence through sex.

In Israel, "The Institute" is the Mossad. A *katsa* is a case officer. A *mabuah* is a non-Jewish informer, a *kidon* an assassin, an *oter* an Arab spy. You're among the *dardasim* if you operate in China, a *falach* in Lebanon, one of the *safanim* if you're targeting the Palestine Liberation Organization (PLO). A *bodel* is a go-between; a *teud* is a forgery.

The Mossad, some people claim, was behind the 1998 bombings of the U.S. embassies in Kenya and Tanzania, the 2002 Bali nightclub bombing, the 9/11 attacks, the deaths of Robert Maxwell and Princess Di. These tales are almost certainly conspiracy theories, or blow-back—lies fed on purpose to the press. Still, in the 1990s, the CIA identified Israel as one of six foreign countries with "a government-directed, orchestrated, clandestine effort to collect U.S. economic secrets." The case of Jonathan Pollard, the U.S. naval intelligence officer sentenced to life imprisonment for passing thousands of classified military documents to Israel, is well known. It is less well known that a special Israeli Mossad unit code-named "A1" combed Silicon Valley and Boston's Route 128 corridor for high-tech secrets. My father was, in fact, a member of a group of angel investors that worked with Boston-based high-tech start-ups, but the Mossad's A1 unit was not one of the things he told me about that day. I read about it later, in a book.

15

17.

It wasn't until the end of our conversation that my father leaned back in his chair and gave me a crooked grin. "You know," he said, "I did do a lot of work, indirectly, with the Mossad."

So there it was. I didn't even have to ask.

He told me he'd been recruited by an Israeli friend, a client, who introduced him to his handler at the Mossad. "It wasn't cloak-and-dagger stuff," he said, swaggering a bit. "Maybe a degree or two below."

He'd already told me about how he'd traveled to Egypt in the '70s to advise the government on reorganizing the country's rayon mills. "I was lucky the Egyptians didn't find out that I'd served in the Israeli military," he'd said. "I had to rush to get a new U.S. passport, one without an Israeli stamp. They thought I was just another American businessman. It was a good thing, too, because as it happened, I was in Alexandria when my old unit, Shayetet 13, made an attack and sank two Egyptian ships."

Now I tried to picture my father in Alexandria, looking out over the famous harbor at the sinking ships. Had he sent a cryptic telegram, placed a secret call?

"No, no," he said, flicking his hand dismissively and tsking the way Israelis did. "I wasn't involved in anything like that."

So what information *did* he provide to the Mossad? "Oh, economic information, mostly." Like what? "Like what kinds of industries different countries had, where they were investing, what installations they had, things like that."

I sighed. "What's the deal with those Saudis, anyway?"

"Oh, them," he said. Another flick, another frown. "They're gone." Gone? "They moved." Moved? "They were thrown out." And what had he been doing with them, anyway? "They wanted to build bridges between Israel and

Syria." Bridges? What kind of bridges? "They wanted to get Israeli companies to set up subsidiaries in Cyprus to market medical products to Syria." Why? "They wanted to barter for stuff in defense and electronics." Well, what happened? "Oh, they just did a lot of monkey business, in the end."

18.

I wrote the essay about my dad. My husband and my friends thought it was funny. A small literary journal picked it up. Not long after the issue appeared, I got an email from my father. He wrote:

> *I have been informed by my Mossad contacts that you published a story 'Secret Agent Man' in the Third Coast spring 05 issue. The Mossad claims it might jeopardize my future cover. Was the story published as they claim??*

I read the email twice. Then I freaked out. I cried. I blamed my husband. I blamed myself. What had I done? What should I do? I didn't really believe I'd blown his cover. But I felt that I'd betrayed him anyway. I didn't want to think about how he would react when he read what I had written: the louche descriptions, the fun I'd poked at his posturing and fibs, the outing of his toupee, worst of all.

I replied to my father's email. *It's classified information, sorry!* I wrote. I clicked Send. I thought I was being clever. My husband and I laughed.

But a message from my father was waiting in my inbox the next morning, informing me that he'd sent a check for $8.00 to *Third Coast* magazine and that he looked forward to receiving a copy in the mail.

I didn't get it. How could my father, who read nothing but newspapers and spy novels, have found out about that essay? *Third Coast* had a circulation of less than a thousand copies. You had to subscribe. It was not available in stores. It was not available online.

And then it clicked. *Online.* I typed my name into Google, just as I had shown my father, and there it was, on *Third Coast*'s website: "Margot Singer's essay explores with childlike awe and adult suspicion the mysterious life of the author's father," the blurb about the current issue read.

The weeks ticked by. My father didn't say anything about the essay. My mother didn't either. I figured he'd kept it a secret from her, too.

Finally, my father called. "I read that story you wrote about me," he said. He paused, then said, "You got some of your facts wrong, but you write very well."

I felt awful. His praise made me feel even worse.

We didn't speak of it again for years.

19.

My father announced that he wanted to write his memoirs, but he was frustrated that he couldn't type. I tried to teach him how to use a Dictaphone, the voice-recognition feature on his Mac. When that didn't work, I suggested he narrate his stories to me. I showed him how easy it would be for me to record him speaking on my iPhone, then transcribe the notes. We gave it a shot, but his heart didn't seem to be in it, and after one or two attempts, we quit.

Instead, he made a detailed outline. On one of my visits to Boston, he handed it to me and then called me into the dining room, where he had spread an array of documents across the table: newspaper and journal articles, business reports, conference papers, exhibition postcards, an artsy French record-album cover, fabric swatches, photographs, a couple of expired Israeli passports. He made me take pictures with my phone of all the items he'd laid out.

"There," he said, when I was done. "Now you can write a book!"

But what book, I wondered, would that be? The objects were an accounting, of sorts, of his professional accomplishments, evidence of his expertise, of his successful (and less successful) business ventures, the money he'd made, the impact he'd had. But what was missing were the *details,* and without them the artifacts could not be brought to life. Where were the stories? Where were the people? Where, more to the point, were my mother, my brother, me?

20.

My father stayed healthy and sharp through his late eighties, but slowly, inevitably, he changed. He suffered from the ignominy of dentures and the pain of gouty arthritis and neuropathy on the bottom of his feet. He needed eye drops for glaucoma. He had a pacemaker implanted in his chest.

The year he turned eighty-nine, after more than half a century of concealment, he took off his toupee. He surprised us when we met up for a family vacation in Florida, pulling off his baseball cap at the Fort Myers airport for a dramatic reveal. My husband, who had also gone bald very young, laughed and shook my father's hand, as did our kids, but I didn't like it. The smooth, pale skin of my father's scalp, hidden for all those years, looked vulnerable and strange. It wasn't that he looked older, exactly; he just didn't look like himself.

Forty-four years had passed since the day Lynnie passed me that note in Latin class. In all that time, no one in our family had ever uttered the word *toupee.* I wondered what made us so protective of his secret, why we let him hide his head. Maybe we wanted to give him the grace of one small vanity. Maybe we couldn't bear to see him age.

I couldn't bear it, anyway. I wanted him to stay the way he'd always been, the father of my childhood, as dashing and invulnerable as Secret Agent Man John Drake.

21.

About two years before he died, my father sent me an email. It said, *Can you Email me the story? thanks.*

What story? I wrote back, although of course I knew. *The* story, the one I wished I hadn't written, the one he'd sent away for and that we'd never talked about again.

My father said he wanted a copy of the essay to send to my cousin's son, who was interviewing my father for an assignment he was working on for a college class.

I took a breath. I said, "So, Dad, you know how when you first read that essay, you told me I'd gotten some of my facts wrong?" My face felt hot. "Which facts, exactly, did I get wrong?"

"Well," my father said. He cleared his throat. "The truth is, I really did do some work for the Mossad."

"Oh," I said. "Okay."

"I didn't do any real *spying*," he said. "I provided some economic information. Nothing major. I just piddled around."

"Oh," I said again. I was touched by his humility. I didn't know what to think.

There was a pause, and then he said, "That is the truth."

"Okay," I said.

I wanted to know more, but I asked no more questions. I'm not sure what else he would have told me, or what difference it would have made. We left it at that.

GOD'S EYE

Many years ago, I lived on the thirtieth floor of an Upper West Side high-rise in New York. It was a crappy apartment with a picture-postcard view. From the living room and bedroom windows, you could watch the helicopters buzzing back and forth along the Hudson, the ferries and the cruise ships gliding past. I had no idea what I was looking at beyond the river (Weehawken? Hoboken? Secaucus?), but it didn't matter. The view made it feel as if I was flying. To the west, the sun flamed and sank behind the far rim of New Jersey. To the south, the city stretched into a circuit board of lights.

I rented the apartment without considering the inconvenience of having to ride the elevator thirty floors to do a load of laundry or run an errand. I didn't think about what I'd do if the power failed or the elevator broke. I didn't worry about what would happen if there were a fire. I didn't care that the walls were thin and that the appliances were old and cheap. I'd moved back to New York after breaking up with the man I'd thought I was going to marry. I looked out at the view and knew the apartment was the one for me.

Who isn't drawn to the view from high places? The scenic overlook, the rooftop terrace, the lookout tower, the observation deck? Tourists queue for hours to see what can be seen from the top of the Empire State Building, the Eiffel Tower, the Burj Khalifa, the Space Needle, Top of the Rock. We thrill to the stomach-dropping high-speed elevators, labor up the claustrophobic, winding flights of stairs. We snap selfies, squint through coin-operated binoculars, pick out landmarks if we can. We crowd close up against the glass or railings, look down and relish the spine-tingling gut-twist of great height.

But what is it, really, that draws us to a view? Is it a vestige of the evolutionary advantage of claiming the highest point? Or is it just a way to transcend our human puniness, if only for a moment? What do you gain? What can you really see?

*

The first aerial photographs were taken from cameras rigged to carrier pigeons, balloons, rockets, kites. In 1858, Nadar shot the first successful aerial photograph from a hot-air balloon tethered 262 feet above Paris. Two years later, James Wallace Black repeated the stunt in Boston, shooting what's now the oldest surviving aerial photograph from a balloon 2,000 feet above the North End. In 1878, Eadweard Muybridge made his first famous photo-panoramic montage from the observation tower of a mansion atop San Francisco's California Street.

To the Victorians, the God's-eye vision was a marvel and a shock. The grayscale vistas captured by the camera were broader than anything that could be seen from the bell tower of a cathedral or an outcropping of rock. And what the photographs made manifest was not God's creation, but mankind's: the miniature houses, the tiny ships moored to matchstick wharves, the toy-size steepled churches and chimneyed factories, the patterned grids of streets. Due to the large format plates and long exposure times, the streets in the photographs are empty, all human life erased. The grainy cityscapes look like an architect's model: perfect, frozen, fake.

A photograph, as Oliver Wendell Holmes once put it, is a "mirror with a memory." At first an emblem of futuristic progress, those pioneering aerial photographs now give us back the vanished past: Paris as it was before Haussmann's transformations in the 1850s and '60s, Boston before the Great Boston Fire of 1872, San Francisco before the 1906 earthquake. The shock and marvel, from our perspective, lie in the vantage point of time, not distance. Those cities and their inhabitants have long since vanished, but the images persist, miraculous as saintly visions captured in ions of 150-year-old light on plates of silver-halide-coated glass.

*

Today, thousands of satellites pass overhead each hour—disembodied eyes in space. They watch us, and we watch what they see. On the NASA website, in real time, you can track the cloud banks as they swirl around the globe, follow the shadow-edge of day as it fades into night. With a click of the mouse, you can see the spreading smoke from wildfires, phytoplankton blooms in Arctic waters, spiral vortices of hurricanes, bursts of sulfurous volcanic ash.

Like those first nineteenth-century aerial photographs, the satellite images show not only God's but man's creations: highways cutting across deserts, bridges linking islands, bright dendritic clusters of nocturnal city lights. You can't actually make out the Great Wall of China, but you can see the ancient pyramids at Giza, the temples in the jungle at Cambodia's Angkor Wat. You can't miss the scabby swaths of deforestation, mining hotspots, oil slicks, blue-green whorls of melting glacial ice.

The images the satellites beam back are revelation, warning, proof. They hold up a mirror; they both magnify and shrink. *There you are*, they say: a speck of carbon on a marble, spinning recklessly through space.

*

I met the man I thought I was going to marry in the fall after I finished college. We were students in the same graduate program at Oxford, and we sat next to each other on the first day of class. He was tall and runner-thin and kind. He was six years older than I. He had an air of gentle, stable confidence that I trusted from the start.

I'd come to England on a prestigious scholarship, and I was supposed to be having the time of my life, but I was not. I felt alone and miserable, inadequate and lost. I missed my friends, my parents, the boyfriend whom I'd left behind. My Oxford rooms were cold and dingy. New friends seemed hard to make. Since there was a multiyear wait to get a phone, I placed expensive calls to my boyfriend from the BT phone box by the Martyr's Memorial in St. Giles. I sobbed into the receiver. I didn't want to be tethered to a long-distance relationship, but I didn't want to lose it either. I wanted—well, I knew not what.

We got together on a wet night that first December. After a study-group session that involved more drinking than studying, we found ourselves weaving, arm in arm, through the misty city streets at two a.m.. The Emperors looked down at us from atop their columns around the Sheldonian, the Muses from the rooftop of the Bodleian across the street, the gargoyles and grotesques from their perches on the walls along New College Lane.

"Isn't this amazing?" he said, pulling me close. "Can you believe we're here?" At the pavilion by the playing fields, cold hands beneath each other's rain-damp sweaters, we kissed. I felt guilty, needy, grateful. A crack had opened up, and joy flowed in.

That spring and summer, we went on long runs together in the University Parks, rowing on the Thames. We traveled to London and to Cambridge, to the southern coast of England, to the Soviet Union and France. Still, I clung to my long-distance boyfriend. I hid my infidelity and closed my eyes to his. I continued to write him letters, to call him on the phone. I filled one notebook after another with my confusion, angst, and shame.

I can't bear to read those journals now, filled with overwrought, conflicted feelings spelled out in tidy, looping script. How out of control I felt. How little I knew myself.

*

Fairy-tale princesses are sent to high places to protect their virtue, for their safety, or as punishment. They're locked away by controlling fathers, jealous husbands, political authorities, evil ogres, fairies, witches. It's an old, familiar story. "Rapunzel," recorded by the Brothers Grimm in 1812 and Americanized by Disney in 2010, is the version we know best, but the "Maiden in the Tower" archetype dates back to the folklore of tenth-century Persia and seventeenth-century Italy, Greece, and France.

The fairy-tale tower, scholars say, is like a harem or a convent—a space where women are hidden, an instrument of patriarchy. The tower is impregnable: its primary function is to prevent a woman from getting pregnant or to conceal an illegitimate pregnancy. Its phallic shape may explain why girls in fairy tales are so often locked away in towers instead of fortresses or dungeons (surely a more pragmatic choice). The demonstration of power is the point. Paradoxically, a princess hidden in a tower is in fact on full display for all to see. Fairy-tale towers also almost always have a window: an opening, a hole. In this sense, the tower is both male and female, impregnable and pregnable at the same time. The maiden is a vessel locked inside a vessel, waiting to be breached.

The window in Rapunzel's tower, which has no door or stairs, is not like a window in a prison. There are no bars or grille. It's high off the ground but cut low enough in the wall that she can easily see out. Rapunzel can't escape from the "tiny little window at the very top" of her tower, but it lets the witch and prince climb in.

All of the illustrations of the tale are drawn from the

perspective of the prince. There's Rapunzel, leaning out of the open window, or perching on the ledge. There she is looping her prodigious braid over the window's hasp, smiling down upon the prince. The prince is leering up at her. She's his waiting prize, his gift.

*

World War I turned aerial photography into a weapon. Reconnaissance images shot from cameras mounted on low-flying, open-cockpit planes revealed enemy trenches, machine-gun emplacements, artillery movements, ammunition depots, observation posts. Between 1914 and 1918, the British Royal Flying Corps shot millions of photographs, developing them in hours in makeshift tented darkrooms near the front. Cartographers used the photographs to make trench maps, topographical maps, mosaic maps, stereoscopic maps, artillery maps, officers' planning maps. The maps, and the enemy positions noted on them, could be updated daily. For the first time, military intelligence was available almost in real time.

This information gave a huge advantage to the Allies. "I visited some French guns during the *tir de démolition* phase," H. G. Wells wrote in 1917 after spending time with the Third Army Topographical Section on the Western Front. "I counted nine aeroplanes and twenty-six kite balloons in the air at the same time. There was nothing German visible in the air at all. It is a case of eyes and no eyes." In fact, Allied gunners could now hit targets that they couldn't even see.

Still, the aerial images were not easy to decipher. "An air photograph to an inexperienced eye is not a very illuminating thing," Wells observed. "One makes out roads, blurs of wood, and rather vague buildings." Geographers and archaeologists had to be brought in to interpret the barely discernible variations in terrain, the faintest gradations of shade and light.

26

The aerial view flattened the landscape into a diagram. Like the first aerial photographs, the military reconnaissance shots erased the people. "One could hardly believe the trenches were full of men, they looked so peaceful and lifeless," a soldier in the Third Army Maps unit noted in a letter home. As the poet W. H. Auden wrote in his essay "Hic et Ille" in 1956:

> From the height of 10,000 feet, the earth appears to the human eye as it appears to the eye of the camera; that is to say, all history is reduced to nature. . . . I cannot distinguish between an outcrop of rock and a Gothic cathedral, or between a happy family playing in a backyard and a flock of sheep, so that I am unable to feel a difference between dropping a bomb upon one or the other.

All history is reduced to nature. Auden understood that God's eye both reveals and erases meaning. Borders and divisions shrink to nothing the farther away you get. How much easier it is to destroy and kill when you can't tell the difference between a rock and a cathedral, a person and a sheep.

*

My grandfather was an Austro-Hungarian officer in the Great War. In a framed photograph that once hung in my grandparents' flat in Haifa, he stands sober and unsmiling in his gray uniform, looking, like all the soldiers of that era, much older than the nineteen-year-old boy he was. A dusty edelweiss, insignia of the elite Austrian mountain troops, is pressed behind the glass.

My grandfather was stationed in the mountains along the Italian front. There in the Dolomites, the opposing forces set iron bolts and rungs into forty-degree slopes and strung cableways across sheer limestone faces, moving men and mortars, flamethrowers and ammunition, food and water into precarious positions along the 10,000-foot peaks. Though less well known than the trench warfare in the west, the battles fought in Italy were among the deadliest of the entire First World War. More than a million men lost their lives. They died in artillery bombardments, avalanches, mortar attacks, rockfalls, of typhoid fever, poison gas, sniper fire, freezing temperatures, the Spanish flu.

My grandfather rarely spoke about the war, although I remember one story about how his mother back in Brno managed to send him çakes, and how in the killing cold of winter, the newspapers in which the cakes were wrapped saved his and his men's feet. Only once, my boyfriend drew him out. Hunched together at a table in the lobby of a hotel, my grandfather sketched diagrams on a scrap of paper, and my boyfriend listened and asked the questions that none of us had ever thought to ask. I don't remember much of what they talked about, just the place names "Rozes" and "Grappa." Or I think I do, at least.

Online, I learn about the infamous 1915–16 standoff at the Castelletto, a 700-foot-high rock tower abutting the Tofana di Rozes massif that controlled a key supply route through the Alps. For months, German and Austrian snipers positioned atop the crag picked off the Italian troops below. Crack Italian Alpini mountain troops attempted to climb the tower with hemp ropes and ladders, shot at it from facing ledges, bombarded it with artillery. When all that failed, they dug a 1,650-foot-long tunnel underneath the tower, packed it with 70,000 pounds of explosives, and blew up the Austrian platoon—along with half of their own men.

I read, too, about the three ferocious battles fought in 1917 and 1918 at Monte Grappa. I click on pictures of the memorial complex built in 1935 that stretches across the summit now. Six massive stone terraces descend from a ridgetop chapel in ever-widening concentric rings, their

Fascist grandeur cutting a jarring contrast to the jagged Dolomitic peaks. Arched niches cut into the curving terrace walls contain the remains of the more than 12,000 Italian servicemen who died fighting on the peak. A second nearby ossuary houses the remains of the 10,000 Austro-Hungarian soldiers who also perished on the site.

My grandfather was too young to have experienced the standoff at the Tofana di Rozes, but he might well have been at Monte Grappa for the final battle in the terrible autumn of 1918. I imagine him standing on that ridgeline as, perhaps, just for a moment, the fog and storm clouds cleared. He would have looked out onto the same panorama you'd see there now: the flatlands of the Venetian plain, the brown curve of the Piave river, the far blue smudge of the Adriatic Sea.

How peaceful—how unreachable—how impossible—it must have seemed.

*

In cities around the world today, a billion CCTV cameras keep watch from rooftops, the sides of buildings, traffic signals, streetlamp poles. They watch us as we move through airports, office buildings, sports arenas, factories, bus and subway stations, malls and shops. Motion sensors trigger the cameras to start recording; software continuously analyzes the footage, scanning for suspicious patterns, then alerting the police.

Surveillance cameras mounted on drones are used by law enforcement agents, environmental scientists, movie directors, land-use planners, advertising agencies, and spies. The MQ-1B Predator drone comes loaded with infrared sensors, daylight and image-intensified TV cameras, a laser designator, a laser illuminator. Through a satellite transponder, it can transmit a live, full-motion video feed. It can stay aloft for more than twenty hours at a time. The even more sophisticated MQ-9 Reaper can pick out an object the size of a milk carton from an altitude of 30,000 feet. Even the DelFly Micro drone, the shape and size of a dragonfly, is capable of taking pictures during flight.

About one-third of all U.S. military aircraft are drones. Drone pilots, stationed on bases halfway around the globe from their targets, fly missions the way you play a video game, manipulating joysticks, tracking hits on screens. Armed with Hellfire air-to-ground missiles and laser-guided bombs, the hunter-killer Reaper drones are assassination machines. So are Switchblade drones, which carry a small warhead and can be programmed to destroy targets up to seven miles away. Even commercial-grade drones can pinpoint and blow up sensors, communications infrastructure, armored vehicles and tanks. Swarms of tiny microdrones, guided by AI, adapt to evolving conditions in real time.

Still, drones are notoriously imprecise, not because their aim is bad (it's not), but because the intelligence on which the strikes are based is very often flawed. Between 2010 and 2020, American drones carried out more than 14,000 strikes in Afghanistan, Pakistan, Yemen, and Somalia. As many as 17,000 people—many of them civilians and children—were likely killed, although it's hard to know for sure. The numbers remain as abstract as they were in Auden's time, the carnal cost unreal.

*

According to the (probably apocryphal) hagiographies, Saint Barbara was locked inside a tower by her father, a wealthy pagan nobleman, to keep her safe from suitors until he could arrange a lucrative marriage. But Barbara didn't want to get married. She secretly converted to Christianity instead. When Barbara's father discovered her heresy, he grabbed her by the hair and hauled her before the authorities. They condemned her to death, and her father drew his sword and sliced off his own daughter's head. God took Barbara's side, of course: a bolt of lightning promptly struck her father dead.

Offering protection from lightning, fire, and explosions, the martyr Barbara is the patron saint of sappers, miners, armorers, military engineers, mathematicians, and artillerymen. Her statue sits deep in the salt mines of Wieliczka, Poland; on the colonnade of St. Peter's Basilica in Rome; on the Charles Bridge in Prague; on the rooftop of the Academy of Mines and Metallurgy in Kraków. She is usually portrayed holding a three-windowed tower, a symbol of the Holy Trinity.

In 1940, occupying Nazi troops threw the statue of Saint Barbara off the roof of the Academy. A reconstruction was installed in 1999. Nearly seven meters tall, Saint Barbara once again gazes blindly over Kraków from her rooftop throne, her mannish expression placid as a Buddha's. A Bible lies open on her left thigh. She holds a crenellated tower, like a giant phallus, or a child, on the right.

*

We talked about getting married only once, at the end of our second year in England. We'd finished our degrees, and I'd accepted a job with a management consulting firm in New York. He was planning to stay on in England for a few more months, freelancing for the newspaper he'd worked for before graduate school, although he was hopeful that a position in their New York City bureau would open up at some point. For the second time in two years, I faced another transatlantic move, another long-distance relationship. I told myself that it would be all right.

I spent a month in Switzerland on a training program for my new firm, and he met me there when it wrapped up. We rented a car and drove south to Nice, then east along the

Riviera. We stopped for a couple of days in Portofino, where we ate pesto and peaches and hiked the steep, pine-scented trails to San Fruttuoso and Santa Margherita. On our last evening, by a bench alongside the yacht-filled harbor, he said he wanted to marry me.

My face burned, and anxiety trilled inside my heart. I mumbled something about not being ready, and he said he didn't expect an answer. That he knew I was still young and had a lot to figure out. That he just wanted me to know the way he felt. He didn't give me a ring. Nothing was official. But it was clear we'd crossed a line—a line that stretched from that bench in Portofino out across the Mediterranean and into the hazy future, to the home and family and life together that we'd create.

I was twenty-three. Excited as I was to be starting my "real" life, I wasn't at all sure I wanted to move alone to New York City and launch a challenging career in a field I feared I wouldn't like. But I was certain my parents wouldn't want me to get married. They wanted me to come back to the States. They were thrilled about the job I'd taken. Besides, I'd already signed a contract, completed a month of training, and cashed in my signing bonus to pay for this very trip. I felt locked into a plan from which there could be no escape.

That night, I remember looking out over the harbor as the sun bled into the sea and darkness draped the hills. Soon I couldn't see beyond the harbor, just as I couldn't imagine any future other than that which others had set out for me. All I really wanted was for the moment we were in to never end. I wanted to go back to our hotel room and make wild love and never get out of bed again.

On Google Maps, you can still zoom in on that bench beside the Portofino harbor. We are long gone, of course. The moment missed.

*

The surface of the earth is a palimpsest, a text repeatedly written over and erased. But traces of the past can be read like hieroglyphics, if you know where and how to look. More than a century after the First World War, aerial images of the Western Front still reveal the dimpled impressions left by bombs, crop marks created by water pooling in the long-abandoned trenches underground. The earth gives up its relics. Each spring, farmers ploughing their fields in Belgium and France still turn up an "iron harvest" of unexploded ordnance, shrapnel, barbed wire, bullets, shards of bone. Melting Alpine glaciers offer gas masks, goggles, boots, howitzers, even photographs, long preserved in ice.

Inspired by his experience as an observer in the British Royal Flying Corps during the war, pioneering field archaeologist Osbert G. S. Crawford flew over Wessex in 1924, taking photographs from a de Havilland DH.9 with a camera captured from the Germans. From 4,000 feet up, he identified what one could only guess at from below: Bronze Age barrows, Iron Age ramparts, Celtic lynchets, Roman camps. Surveying the landscape from the air, Crawford wrote, was like looking at a halftone photograph in the newspaper. What up close appears to be nothing but a maze of dots resolves, with distance, into a sharper image. Prehistoric drainage pits and ditches showed up as belts of darker green, where the crops grew lusher in the moist silt where the chalk down had been disturbed hundreds of years ago. Daisies and poppies marked the spots with white and scarlet rings.

Today, Crawford would no doubt be thrilled to learn, thermal and infrared images shot from a drone reveal 2,000-year-old artifacts that are completely invisible to the human eye. Carbon dating, DNA analysis, geochemistry, drone imaging, and space telescopes continue to offer new perspectives and insights into the history of the earth. But there's still so much we cannot understand, so much we don't know how to see.

*

I wanted to be an archaeologist when I was a kid. We spent a few weeks most summers visiting my father's family in Israel, and in those days, Roman coins still sometimes washed up on the beaches, and Yigael Yadin was a national hero. My mother gave me books: a biography of the archaeologist Heinrich Schliemann, the British Museum catalogue from the blockbuster 1972 Tutankhamun exhibition she'd queued up to see, James A. Michener's novel *The Source*. The summer I was eleven, I sat by the pool at the Dan Carmel hotel in Haifa and slogged through all 1,000 pages of Michener's tome. In Acre and Caesarea and Jerusalem, we walked past real-life digs. I watched the volunteers at work, crouched beneath the sun, bucket hats on their heads, as they sifted trays of sand, brushed off bits of clay or stone. I peered at the fragments of low walls and trenches, at the areas of dirt staked off with string. I tried to imagine the Crusader church, the Roman storeroom, or the Israelite dwelling described on the signs posted at the site, but I was inevitably disappointed. All you could really see was dirt and rubble. Still, I was fascinated by the idea that the past could be pieced together like a puzzle, that buried history could be reclaimed.

Archaeology appealed to me, maybe, because my own family's history was so full of gaps and blanks. None of the places my relatives came from were on the Rand McNally map my sixth-grade teacher pulled down like a window shade on the classroom wall. I searched in vain for *Austria-Hungary, Czechoslovakia, Lithuania, Galicia, Palestine*. War had wiped away the countries, borders, names. My father's family had fled from Brno to Haifa, my mother's from Alytus, Lithuania to Portland, Maine. A few distant cousins whom I'd never met were scattered from Hartford to Vancouver, London to Tel Aviv. I could count all my closest living relatives—two grandparents, three uncles, five first cousins—on the fingers of my two hands.

So much was lost in translation. My father couldn't remember any of the Czech he'd spoken before they fled. My mother couldn't remember much of the Yiddish her grandfather had taught her as a child. My grandparents spoke German with each other, Hebrew with my Israeli cousins, English with my mom and brother and me. My cousins and I communicated in a semi-incoherent mix of broken English and body language. I took Latin and French in high school, but my own family story remained as unintelligible as the Hebrew I never learned to read or speak.

*

Freud, famously, was fascinated by archaeology. His consulting rooms at Berggasse 19 in Vienna, and later at 20 Maresfield Gardens in London, were filled with artifacts. Bronze statuettes and terra-cotta figurines of ancient gods stood two rows deep along his writing desk, in glassed-in cabinets, on tabletops and bookshelves: Isis, Athena, Artemis, Imhotep, Buddha, Venus, Eros, Thoth. A print of the temple of Ramses II at Abu Simbel hung above the couch. On the facing wall was the famous picture of the Sphinx.

Schliemann's excavations of Troy in the 1870s gave Freud and his fellow late-Victorians the first scientific evidence that Homer's and Virgil's famous tales were based on real historical events. Similarly, the early excavations in Jerusalem undertaken by the British explorers Edward Robinson, Charles Warren, and Charles Wilson offered seemingly miraculous verification of the Hebrew Bible. Here was Hezekiah's Tunnel! There was the Jebusite City of David, there the Temple Mount! The ancient scriptures were no longer merely stories, but hard facts grounded in the stones and earth.

Freud saw in archaeology a metaphor for the analytic process. Just as the archaeologist dug up ancient ruins, so the psychoanalyst uncovered the primal drives and memories buried deep within the patient's unconscious mind. In their 1895 *Studies on Hysteria*, Freud and Breuer compared psychoanalysis to "the technique of excavating a buried city." Like archaeologists "clearing away the pathogenic psychical material layer by layer," they wrote, the analyst helped the patient piece together memories and meanings unknown and often unacceptable to the patient's conscious self. From his vantage by the couch, the analyst traced patterns in the patient's associations, linguistic double meanings, slips of the tongue, memories, and dreams. Slowly, the repressed returned. Slowly, a narrative cohered.

*

I turned twenty-four and moved to New York City. Just six months later, my boyfriend's newspaper offered him his dream job as their European bureau chief. My vision of us living together in New York evaporated in a blink. I didn't consider asking him to choose me over his career. After all, I wasn't sure I even liked my job or living in the city. I requested a transfer to my firm's London office, instead. I resolved to fit my life to his.

But by the time I finally moved back to England, one very long year later, nothing felt right. I hung my suits and blouses in the half of the narrow bedroom closet he'd cleared out for me, stacked my books beside his on the shelves. I tried not to think about the guy I'd had a fling with just a few weeks before I left. From the flat's second bedroom, my boyfriend filed dispatches to his editors and planned reporting trips to exciting-sounding places. I put on a suit and took the Tube to my firm's Knightsbridge office, where I put in the long hours I'd grown used to in New York.

I was staffed on projects for an insurance company, a fast-food conglomerate, a telecom provider. The men I worked with—and they were almost all men—criticized me for not being aggressive enough or for being too aggressive, told me to get them coffee, laughed when I complained about staying up all night to meet the unreasonable deadlines they had set. I came home in tears. "You don't have to do this," my boyfriend said, but his kindness stabbed like disapproval, and something deep inside me hardened into a twist. If I left my job, what would I do? Other than his girlfriend, who would I be? I felt that I had something to prove, though to whom I had no idea. I couldn't allow myself to quit.

The closeness I'd yearned for from a distance now felt like shackles. Darkness swarmed inside my head. I wrote angry, anguished entries in my journal. I fought with my boyfriend. He urged me to "see someone," by which he meant a shrink. My mother, a veteran of psychoanalysis, encouraged me as well.

Thus I found myself making up excuses to skip out on work four times a week and dash across town to the British Institute of Psychoanalysis on Harley Street, where I spent fifty minutes lying on a cot and . . . talking. It didn't make me feel much better—not right away, at least. The self-discoveries Freud promised, I came to see, were no easier to decipher than the rubble-filled archaeological sites I'd seen in Israel as a child, or the grainy World War I photographs of trenches taken from the air. Digging down into the self is a slow and messy process. It's murky, ambiguous, inefficient, weird. It's dark down there, disturbing, full of shame. Dreams distort and skip. There are no truths but riddles. You only know you're onto something when you begin to weep.

37

*

I first watched Charles and Ray Eames' nine-minute 1977 documentary film, *Powers of Ten,* in high school. Designed to show "the relative size of things in the universe and the effect of adding another zero," the film opens with the image of a couple sitting on a picnic blanket in Chicago's Burnham Park on an October day. The opening shot is one meter wide; the camera is one meter away. Every ten seconds, the camera moves ten times farther away and the field of view grows ten times wider. After reaching the farthest-known reaches of the universe—the blank, black space at 100,000,000 light-years (10^{24})—the film reverses, zipping back to the couple on their picnic blanket in Chicago, then zooming inward by one power of ten every ten seconds, into a single cell. It stops at 0.000001 angstroms (10^{-16}) within the gray, vibrating chaos of a single proton's core.

Not long ago, I found the film on YouTube and watched it again and again. I was struck by the almost mystical symmetry of the exponents, the patterns of light and darkness, crowdedness and space. I was amazed by the similarity of the swarm of electrons inside the carbon atom's nucleus (10^{-10}) to the Milky Way's spiral swirl of stars (10^{10}). *Here you are*, the numbers said: twenty-four zeros from the farthest reaches of the cosmos, sixteen zeros from a quark.

Photography, archaeology, and psychoanalysis emerged at nearly the same moment in the middle of the nineteenth century, forever changing the way we saw the world and thought about ourselves. At the dawn of the scientific-technical revolution, the discoveries held such promise: Reality could be caught on film, the past dug up and reconstructed, critical perspective gained. But today, psychoanalysis has given way to pharmacology, and digital imaging and AI have frayed the line between what is real and what is fake. A friend writes: "How can we look inside an atom or outward to the universe when we can't even look inside ourselves?"

In 2021, *Star Trek* actor William Shatner became, at ninety, the oldest person to travel into space. Shatner said he thought the trip on Jeff Bezos's *Blue Origin* space shuttle would be cathartic, a "next beautiful step to understanding the harmony of the universe." But what he felt looking back on Earth's blue marble was neither awe nor beauty. Instead, "it was among the strongest feelings of grief I have ever encountered. The contrast between the vicious coldness of space and the warm nurturing of Earth below filled me with overwhelming sadness." One hundred kilometers above the Earth, he found himself face-to-face with death.

*

After we broke up, I moved from London to that thirtieth-floor apartment in New York, and the man I'd thought I was going to marry moved to Berlin. He sent me a letter along with a photograph of himself standing on a city street. He had on an overcoat and gloves and looked a little hunched and stiff. Things were not going well with the German woman he was dating. This was not the life he'd wanted, he said.

Out my window, I watched the moving leaden water of the Hudson and thought about the bombed-out church tower that Berliners call *der hohle Zahn*, "the hollow tooth." Kaiser Wilhelm's tower had been left in ruins as a reminder of the destruction of the war. Our failed love, too, felt like the hole left by a lost tooth that you can't stop touching with your tongue. Even though I was the one who'd ruined everything, I missed him. Despite my years of psychoanalysis, I still didn't understand why I had done it—why I hadn't let our story end the way we'd hoped it would.

What did I want? Why was it so hard to tell? Where

was it, my authentic life, the one not set out for me by anybody else? I knew it had to be out there somewhere—beyond the Hudson, beyond New Jersey, beyond any feature of the landscape I could see—but I couldn't picture it. The future—my desire—remained as cold and dark as Shatner's space.

*

I had forgotten the ending to "Rapunzel." I thought the prince climbed up Rapunzel's braid and set her free. But, in fact, when the prince climbs up that final time, it's not Rapunzel he finds waiting at the top, but her evil guardian, the witch. The witch has chopped off Rapunzel's hair, banished her to the wilderness. It is a trap, a trick. The crone shoves the prince out of the tower window, and he falls into a snarl of briars. The thorns poke out his eyes, and he goes blind.

For years, the blind prince wanders through the forest, until one day, he hears a familiar voice. It's Rapunzel, who has survived along with the twins—the prince's children—that she gave birth to after being cast out by the witch. Rapunzel runs to the prince, weeping with joy, and as her tears fall into his eyes, "they became clear once again, and he could see."

*

There's no view to speak of out the window by the desk where I now write. There are only brambles, the brown litter of dead leaves, spindly tree trunks and branches, a shred of sky, clouds drifting in the wind. If I'm looking for perspective, I will not find it here.

Eventually, of course, I fell in love again, left consulting, moved across the country, went back to school, began to write. We got married and had two children. They grew up. Our lives keep rippling outward in concentric rings. Somewhere up there in the pale Midwestern sky, passing satellites keep silent watch. The daytime moon looks on, translucent as a dream.

In fairy tales, the hero must get lost, or go blind, before he can find himself. I wish I could say that, as time passed, I too have gained insight, hindsight, knowledge, wisdom. But it's still impossible to see the way ahead. I keep on wandering, searching for that greater height.

THE POWER SUIT

It is boxy, mannish, with shoulder pads fit for a linebacker and a skirt that tapers to below the knee. You pair it with a blouse that ties around your neck in a floppy bow, sheer black pantyhose, pumps that match your purse. Big earrings, big hair. Think Princess Di in the early days. Think Margaret Thatcher, Joan Collins in *Dynasty*, Ivana Trump.

For many years, at the back of my closet, there hung a few relics of my New York City work wardrobe circa 1986. From time to time, I'd pull them out, trying to decide if I should give them away. One of my favorites was a black-and-white houndstooth Christian Dior number. The jacket had big black buttons, black grosgrain trim. I put it on. The skirt no longer buttoned at the waist, but otherwise it fit. I slid on heels and turned before the mirror. I used to dress like this every morning, I reminded myself: pantyhose, pumps, blouse, skirt, jewelry, jacket, coat. On the rare days I wasn't out of town at a client's, I took a cab to work, bought a latte at the kiosk in the lobby of my building—a green-glass skyscraper on 52nd between Madison and Park—and crowded into the elevator along with all the men in their dark suits and white shirts and understated ties. We checked out our reflections in the brass button panel as the elevator rose. We were on our way.

I turned again. The jacket's padded shoulders were ridiculous, really. They'd look even more ridiculous with a cravat-style blouse. I never liked those foppish bows. They always seemed inappropriately girly, a throwback to Victorian femininity—an anxious gesture rather than an aggressive one, a reminder of the incongruity of a woman in a suit.

It seems to me that the female power suit was actually a parody. The Organization Man in drag. Only the joke was not on him.

*

I arrived in New York to interview for jobs with management consulting firms on January 28, 1986, the day the *Challenger* blew up. In my hotel room the next morning, I put on my interview suit. It was a brown-checked cashmere Brioni with a pleated skirt that my father had gotten for me as part of some business dealings with an importer friend. I tucked in a green silk blouse and tied the bow around my neck. I turned in front of the mirror. I didn't recognize myself.

I spent the day in interviews, almost exclusively with men. I ran the numbers on the case-study problems they posed. I told them about my experience serving as the first woman business manager of my college newspaper in its 110-year history. They informed me that nearly one-third of the incoming associates were women and assured me that the partnership would soon reflect those numbers, too.

Before I moved to New York to start the job that spring, I went shopping with my mom. We bought suits: navy pinstripes, gray flannel, basic black. At Ann Taylor, I chose a brown suit with enormous padded shoulders and a shawl collar. At Brooks Brothers, I picked out a lavender linen summer suit. I bought a long navy skirt, a red shirtdress. I bought blouses. I bought pumps. I bought a leather briefcase. I was set.

The only thing I could actually imagine about the job was what I'd look like dressed up in those new clothes. I pictured myself seated at a conference table, my padded shoulders squared, my legs crossed, a cigarette tipped between the fingers of one hand. (I didn't smoke, but still). I saw myself as if from a distance, projected on a screen. But if my future was a film, it was one I'd never seen. My father was the businessman, and the only woman he ever worked with was his secretary, for whom he brought back little presents when we went away on trips. My mother had taught fifth grade in a suburban Boston public school; she was told she had to quit her job when she got pregnant. Her mantra was, "Don't be like me."

*

There were only three women CEOs in the top 500 American companies in 1987, the year that I turned twenty-four and started work. The expression "glass ceiling" had just begun to gain widespread attention, but none of us was close enough to the glass ceiling, back then, to understand that shoulder pads would offer no protection for our heads. We weren't worried, yet, about how we'd negotiate all those bows and buttons if we wanted to have kids.

The job we had was the kind of job that, less than a generation before, had been the exclusive domain of men. But the cohort of associates I was hired with was nearly forty percent women, and we were certain the senior partnership—just four percent female—would catch up in due course. We were well educated, well paid, ambitious, smart. My boyfriend gave me a button that I tacked up on my bulletin board. *I want it all and I want it now*, it read.

By the time I left the firm, a decade later, the shoulder pads and floppy ties had happily gone out of style. By the mid-'90s, most of us were wearing shorter skirts and dresses. One or two of us even braved a pantsuit now and then. But the ranks of women partners, which by then included me, had still not budged past four percent. (There were also just two women CEOs in the Fortune 500.) Most of us were single, and those of us who weren't had stay-at-home spouses or a staff of nannies around the clock, just as all the men did. We took the demands of the job—the hours, the travel, the intensity, the absence of women—for granted. We tailored ourselves to fit.

*

For several years, I worked with a woman who was gay but who had not come out at work. Her partner, whom she referred to in public as her "roommate," and later as her "nanny," stayed home with their four adopted kids. Whenever we had a tough client meeting, we'd wear our most conservative pin-striped suits. We donned our highest heels as well, which brought her to about six feet. "You gotta look 'em in the eye," she said.

Once I made the mistake of not wearing a suit to a meeting with a group of telecom network engineers in Birmingham, Alabama. I wore a bright kelly green dress with a black velvet collar and a row of buttons down the front. The secretary who escorted me to the conference room that morning was the only woman I saw that entire day. She looked me up and down and said, in a thick Southern accent, "You're brave to wear *that* here." I didn't understand what she meant until later. Stammering like a wounded peacock before a room full of hostile men, I felt not brave but stupid. I didn't wear the dress again.

The last time I ever put on a suit, I'd recently given birth and was still nursing around the clock. I'd agreed to facilitate an all-day off-site meeting for a group of dot-com executives negotiating a deal. I chose a pale purple suit from Barneys, with—as the song goes—a short skirt and a long jacket. Feeling pleased that I could even zip the skirt around my postpartum waist, I kissed my husband and my baby girl goodbye and went off to work. The clients (all guys, needless to say) showed up in T-shirts and jeans. At the conference center, there was no place to pump. My breasts grew hard and painful and leaked through my bra and blouse. I cried the whole way home.

46

*

All clothing is a system of signs, as Barthes pointed out. We wear our identities, quite literally, on our sleeves. We construct ourselves in clothes; we wrap ourselves in myth. In our mannish power suits, we women of the '80s covered our bodies with the culture's signs of authority, professionalism, prestige. We covered our bodies and stood out. We covered our bodies and fit in.

The power suit is a costume, camouflage, armor, a straightjacket. The power suit, in any incarnation, is inflexible. You wouldn't cook dinner in a power suit. You wouldn't get down on the floor to build LEGOs with your kids.

In the end, for me at least, the power suit was empty. I shriveled up inside it and blew away.

*

Eventually, it became obvious that I'd never wear my suits again, but I still couldn't bring myself to get rid of them. They were made of fine fabrics that would cost a fortune now, I told myself. I imagined giving them to my daughter for dress-up. "Is this *really* what you used to wear to work, Mommy?" she'd say. "When I grow up, will I be a business woman too?" We'd watch her twirl before the mirror, bird-legged in my too-big heels, and we'd giggle at the thought. And I'd say, wishing, even believing, in that moment, that it might be true: "You can be anything you want to be."

CALL IT RAPE

Still life with man and gun

Three girls are smoking on the back porch of their high school dorm. It's near midnight on a Saturday in early autumn, the leaves not yet fallen, the darkness thick. A man steps out of the woods. He is wearing a black ski mask, a hooded jacket, leather gloves. He has a gun. He tells the girls to follow him, that if they make a noise or run, he'll shoot. He makes them lie face down on the ground. He rapes first one and then the others. He walks away.

It is September 1978. Two of the girls are my classmates; the third is a friend of theirs, visiting for the weekend. As a day student, I hear the news on Monday morning. I am fifteen and, like most of us—good girls at an all-girls' boarding school—my experience of sex so far consists of sweaty slow dances and a few nights of awkward groping and beery kisses with boys I never see again. At the special all-school meeting convened that morning, the headmistress informs us of the security guard that has been hired, the safety lights that soon will be installed. Another woman, a cop or counselor, steps up to the microphone. "Rape is a crime of violence, not sex," she says. She repeats it, like a mantra, to make sure we understand.

I try to picture the girls out there in that ravine behind the dorm, dead leaves and pine needles and dirt cold against their skin. The porch light shining dimly through the trees. The man, the mask and gloves and gun. But there the tableau freezes. I simply can't imagine it: the logistics of it, the lying there, the terrible anticipation, and then. Wasn't there *something* they could have done, I can't help thinking, three on one like that?

The incident does not make me fearful. I'm not afraid

to be home alone in my parents' house, just a few miles down the road. I'm not afraid to walk home from my music lessons along the wooded path that winds around the pond behind my house, or to take the T into Boston by myself. I don't believe that what happened to those girls could happen to me. More precisely, it doesn't even occur to me that it could. I can't make any of it touch me: the powerlessness, the fear, the shame.

A few weeks after the rapes, a man is arrested, a tennis pro from a respected local family. Everyone is shocked, relieved. The girls stay in school. They get over it, or so we all believe.

The word rape comes from

The word "rape" comes from the Latin verb *rapere*: to seize, to take by force, to carry off. Rape, in its original sense, was a property crime, a form of theft. The early Romans famously seized and carried off the Sabine women, being short on wives. Poussin depicts the Sabine women flung over the Romans' shoulders, abandoned infants wailing on the ground, fathers wrestling the soldiers to get their daughters back. But in the center of the canvas, in the midst of all the chaos, a slender, blue-gowned woman seems to be strolling off arm-in-arm with her assailant, her head tilted submissively toward his. The Roman historian Livy records that the Sabine women were advised to "cool their anger and give their hearts to the men who had already taken their bodies." A happy ending for an imperial foundation myth.

Other words come from the same Latin root as "rape": *rapture, ravage, rapt, ravenous, rapacious, ravishing*. Ovid's *Metamorphoses* is filled with stories of ravishing nymphs seized and carried off by rapacious gods: Io, Daphne, Callisto, Europa, Andromeda, Leda, Persephone. (There are more than fifty sexual attacks in Ovid, by one scholar's count.) Correggio paints Io in an erotic swoon, her head tipped back, her lips parted, her body one long, sensuous curve of flesh. You might be forgiven for forgetting that Jupiter has just chased her into the woods whereupon, in Ovid's words, "he hid the wide earth in a covering of fog, caught the fleeing girl, and raped her." Titian pictures Europa in a similar state of rapture, sprawled blowsily across the back of a muscular white bull (Jupiter), her fleshy thighs parted, her translucent gown in disarray, a milky breast exposed. Inspired by Titian, Rubens depicts the abduction of the daughters of Leucippus by the twins Castor and Pollux as a Baroque spiral of rearing horses, gleaming armor, flowing golden hair, creamy female skin. The daughters, languidly reaching out for help, do not look exactly happy, but neither do they seem especially distressed.

I read Ovid and studied Roman history in high school. For a Fine Arts course in college, I went to the Isabella Stewart Gardner Museum to see Titian's *Rape of Europa* and Botticelli's *The Story of Lucretia*. I wrote an essay on the aesthetic qualities and cultural contexts of the art. But as far as I can remember, I never considered the fact that these scenes are all depicted from the perspective of a man. It didn't occur to me to ask what it means to glorify sexual violence, to conflate *rapture* and *ravishment* and *rape*.

Cossacks

My mother stands before the bathroom mirror, putting on lipstick, brushing her hair. I am watching her get ready to go out, as I have done since I was a little girl—my beautiful mother with her slender wrists and ankles and thick dark hair. She sprays on her perfume, Hermès' Calèche. Its blend of rose and iris, oak moss, and wood is the essence of my mother, a luxuriant, sexy smell. My father brings her bottles of it when he travels abroad for work.

My mother has hazel eyes, high cheekbones. She brushes rouge onto her cheeks, tilting her face before the mirror. They are a good-looking couple, my parents, romantic, although often enough, they fight. My father mutters curses under his breath when he is angry, hisses syllables hinting at awful names: "*fu----- cu--*," "*stu--- sh--*." He makes all the money and has all the power, my mother complains. She urges me to pursue a career, to be independent, not to marry young the way she did.

My mother inherited her high cheekbones from her mother, she tells me, whose parents emigrated from Czarist Russia at the turn of the century, fleeing the pogroms. My idea of a pogrom comes from *Fiddler on the Roof*—horseback-riding, vodka-swilling Cossacks in belted tunics and leather boots. Who squat and kick their heels out as they dance, their arms folded across their chests. Who rip their sabres through Motel and Tzeitel's down pillows and wedding quilts.

My mother takes a tissue and blots her lips, leaving a coral lip-print kiss. "The Cossacks had high cheekbones," she says. "There must have been some Cossack blood back there, somewhere."

Somehow I understand that she is talking about rape. About the vestiges of that history of violence, helixed like a secret in the DNA of every cell inside her body, and in mine.

Lois Lane

The summer after my first year in college, I get a job working as a reporter for a suburban Massachusetts newspaper, *The Middlesex News*. I am assigned to the Waltham bureau, a dingy storefront office on Moody Street. The editors and reporters sit at metal desks along one side of the room. The opposite side belongs to circulation. Every morning the delivery people (not boys on bikes, but shuffling adults in beat-up cars) file in to deposit their collections, interrupting the buzz and clack of our electric typewriters with the jangle of the coin-sorting machine. I write features on a diner-turned-Chinese restaurant, on neighborhood objections over a cut-down tree, on a museum of industry, on a summer camp for gifted kids. After a few weeks, I am promoted to editorial assistant and assigned the police and court beats.

I have never had a real job before. In the mornings, I sleep too late and arrive at the police station with my wet hair dripping down the back of the skimpy T-shirt or summer dress my mother should have told me not to wear to work. The cops hoot when I approach to read the blotter. They call me Lois Lane.

"Hey, Lois! Howya doin'?" they shout when I walk in, their Boston accents thick. "Where's Clark?"

On Monday mornings, they say, "Hey, Lois, you get married yet?"

I am embarrassed and a little offended but mostly flattered by the teasing. I squirm as I copy into my reporter's notebook the previous day's offenses: vandalized mailboxes, minor drug busts, stolen bikes, toilet-papered trees.

Then in August, there's a rape. The victim, a single woman in her twenties, is awoken at five a.m. by an intruder (*a stocky man with an Italian accent,* I improbably report) who climbs in through her ground-floor bedroom window with a sack over his head. He holds a knife to her throat and threatens to kill her if she makes a sound or tries to run for help.

It's an August heat wave: oppressive, muggy, East Coast heat. Fans whir in the windows of the station house. Sweat trickles down my chest as I stand in the police chief's office, pen in hand, the cover of my reporter's notebook flipped back. He leans back in his desk chair and sighs. He is a heavy man, his collar tight around his ruddy neck. He says, "It's hot. People get crazy, you know, when it's hot."

53

I know only enough to roll my eyes afterward, when I tell people what he said. I do not know that this is the third rape in less than three weeks in Waltham. That the only female rape counselor on the Waltham force was laid off in the last round of budget cuts. That an average of 1.5 women are sexually assaulted in Boston every day. At seventeen, I consider myself a feminist, but I have not read Susan Brownmiller's 1975 book, *Against Our Will*. I have not heard of the slogan "Take Back the Night."

I am Lois Lane. *Wednesday I had a big story—rape!* I write in my diary at the end of the week. *My story made front page on Thursday. It was all very exciting. Went out to dinner with Mom and Dad.*

Denial

I come across a memoir, *Denial*, written by a terrorism expert named Jessica Stern. Stern was fifteen in 1973 when she was raped, along with her fourteen-year-old sister, at gunpoint in her Concord, Massachusetts, home. In 2006, at Stern's request, the Concord police reopened the case files and connected her assault to forty-four other similar rapes in the Boston area. Eighteen of the rapes occurred within an eight-block radius in Harvard Square; victims included the thirteen-year-old daughter of Harvard Law School's dean. Other rapes occurred at nearby boarding schools. Two girls were raped in their dorm at Concord Academy. Two girls were raped at a private school in Natick. Two girls were raped at my high school, Dana Hall.

Whoa, I think. I know this story. That guy—the tennis pro?—raped forty-something other girls as well? But the details do not add up. I remember three girls being raped, not two. Moreover, the man who police say assaulted Stern and her sister was arrested in 1973 and spent the next eighteen years in jail. In 1973, I was ten, not in high school. Have I misremembered what happened? Or did the police make a mistake? Finally, in *The Boston Globe* archives, I find an article detailing the rapes that I remember, dated November 1978. It opens with this lead:

> Lt. Victor Maccini has been a Wellesley policeman for 32 years. His memory faltered the other day when he was asked when his department had conducted its last intensive rape investigation.
>
> He gazed out of his office window and shook his head slowly before answering. "Gee . . . a rape case? I don't remember," he said. "We've had them, though, but they've always been on the outskirts, like Needham or Newton."

But buried a dozen paragraphs down, the same article states:

> Police concede, however, that the case is almost identical to a case in 1971 in which two Dana Hall students reported that they were raped at gunpoint by a masked gunman. That case was never solved.

It takes a minute before I comprehend that we are talking about two different incidents, both at my high school, just seven years apart. Until now, I'd never heard of the 1971 rapes. I can't find a single mention of them in the press. All these years later, I am stunned. So many girls raped, not "on the outskirts," not in the crazy heat of August, but in their homes and dorms, in the tony Boston suburbs where I grew up. I was right there, but I had no idea.

In an op-ed published in *The Boston Globe* in 2010, Amy Vorenberg reveals that she is the girl Stern refers to in her book as "Lucy," the daughter of the Harvard Law School dean, raped in 1971 by a masked gunman in an upstairs bathroom of her mother's house while her family and friends talked and laughed downstairs. The police issued no warning.

55

The next night, the same man raped two more girls just down the street. No one said a thing. "I have been silent long enough," Vorenberg writes. "Although 40 years have passed, respected institutions still suppress information about sexual assault, and rape remains the most under-reported of violent crimes."

The tennis pro, it turned out, was not the rapist. He was acquitted after a short trial at the end of November 1978. The case was never solved.

Red running shorts

It is the end of exam period of my senior year in college. I am finishing a thirty-five-page paper, and I have stretched it right to the end. I sit at my desk, chewing on my pencil, riffling through my stacks of notes, the scribbled pages of my draft. The paper is due at five p.m., and it is already midafternoon, and I have not yet finished writing, have not yet begun to type.

I phone my professor to ask for an extension. Just until the morning, I plead. Just for time to type. I expect him to be sympathetic. I'm a senior, a good student, a hard worker. I've already turned in my honors thesis, passed my orals, won a prestigious scholarship to graduate school. There is a faint buzzing on the line. I wait.

He says, "If that paper is not at my house by nine o'clock tomorrow morning, I'm giving you an F."

Right.

I pull an all-nighter finishing the paper. In the morning, I walk across Harvard Square to the address the professor has given me. It's a long walk; I don't have a car. I haven't showered or changed my clothes. My eyes are gritty, my hair greasy. People are strolling along the sidewalks, new leaves fluttering on the trees, but in my fatigue, nothing feels quite real. I climb the steps and ring the bell.

He comes to the door wearing bright red running shorts and nothing else. He is bare-chested, bare-legged, barefoot, practically naked, except for those red shorts. He is square-jawed and blond-bearded, slim and fit. He motions for me to come in.

I step into the living room. He picks up a telephone that is lying on the table off the hook and, cradling the receiver between his shoulder and his cheek, continues whatever conversation he was having before my arrival as he flips rapidly through the pages of my paper, the one I've worked so hard on, the one I stayed up all night to type. He is skimming, making a show of indifference, I think. He flips the pages, murmuring into the phone. I perch on the edge of the couch and wait. A clock ticks in the kitchen, which I can see through an open door. There is no one else in the house, as near as I can tell. After a little while, he hangs up the phone and fixes me with a look.

"I would have given you an A," he says, "but the paper is late. So I'm giving you a B instead." He comes around the table to me. My heart is beating hard. I'd like to protest—I wrote a thirty-five-page paper, after all, and it is good!—but I do not, cannot, speak.

He writes something on a card, slides it into an envelope. He holds it out to me. "I want you to go over to University Hall now," he says, "and turn in my grades."

Grades are not due for several days, I am quite sure. He has no right to make me run his errands for him. But he is giving me an order, not an option. He stands there in his red running shorts, bare-chested, practically naked, holding out that envelope. It's clear that he would have no compunction about ripping it open and changing the B to an F if I refuse. It's clear he can do anything he wants.

He could, for example, push my head down to those red running shorts and make me suck his dick.

He does not do it, but he could.

I take the envelope and walk back across the Square and turn it in.

Oleanna

Anita Hill is on the radio, promoting her new book. It has been twenty years since the 1991 Senate confirmation hearings in which Hill accused Judge Clarence Thomas of sexual harassment. People are calling in to thank her: women and men who admire her bravery, mothers whose daughters have grown up taking it for granted that it's not okay to tell lewd jokes in the workplace, to touch a woman without asking, to hold out rewards in exchange for sex. I'm thinking of my teenage daughter, what she will encounter soon at school or work. How much has changed?

David Mamet's play *Oleanna*—which I saw at its Harvard Square premiere in 1992, just seven months after the Thomas hearings—dramatizes a power struggle between a college student, Carol, and a young professor, John. Carol is on the verge of failing and desperate to pass John's course. John patronizes Carol's lack of understanding, interrupts their conversation to talk to his wife on the phone, then tells Carol that if she comes to his office for private tutorials, he'll give her an A. In a gesture that might or might not be paternal, John reaches out to touch her shoulder. Carol files a sexual harassment complaint. John's tenure bid is put on hold. When John tries to talk Carol into dropping the charges, he grows angry and grabs her arm, and she raises the charges to attempted rape. In the play's final scene, John loses control and beats Carol with a chair. "Oh, my God," he says, realizing what he has done. From where she cowers on the floor, Carol looks up at him and says slowly, "Yes, that's right."

Mamet complicates the narrative of sexual harassment, giving Carol the power to destroy John, making John both a monster and a dupe. Watching the play, I find that I am shocked that Carol has such power. It has not dawned on me until now that in my own run-in with my red-running-shorts-clad professor, I had power too. (Like John, my professor did not have tenure. All I would have had to do was file a complaint!) Yet I can't help feeling that John, for all his smugness and paternalistic hypocrisy—or, for that matter, my professor—does not deserve to be destroyed. Does power necessarily corrupt? Or are we more complicit in protecting privilege than we'd like to think?

Campus watch

I am now a college professor, the one with power (such as it is) over deadlines, extensions, grades. Since the '80s, of course, many things have changed. I keep my office door open during student conferences, watch my gestures and my language, encourage students to engage with questions of power, privilege, race, gender, class. College is no longer a boys' club. These days, in the classroom, the women outperform the men. They raise their hands and voice opinions. They are diligent, articulate, and bright.

At the college where I teach, as elsewhere, kids drink, hook up. Here, as elsewhere, girls are raped. Girls get drunk at parties and black out and wake up to discover they've been raped. Girls are assaulted walking across campus and in their dorms, by strangers and by friends. A study funded by the U.S. Department of Justice estimates that one in five female students will be raped during their college years. But more than eighty percent of victims do not report the crime.

A former student of mine is one of the few who does speak up. Almost nothing about her case is clear. She says she did shots before going to a party and can't remember anything that happened after that. The boy in question says she came on to him aggressively at a party and clearly wanted sex. She says she only discovered what had happened when she heard the gossip the next day. People who were at the party confirm they saw her grinding with him on the dance floor. After a disciplinary hearing, the boy is suspended for the year. She receives vicious messages, calling her a slut, accusing her of ruining his life.

I don't know what to think. My mother says, "Why should the boy take all the blame? In my day, as a girl, you knew you had to take responsibility for yourself." My husband says, "It's not that complicated. You just don't mess around with a girl who's drunk."

When we meet for coffee, my student says her parents are planning to appeal the verdict; his parents have filed suit. She's looking into transferring to a different college, although so far this semester, her grades are not so great. "It's been pretty rough," she says. She shakes back her long hair and fiddles with her coffee cup. "You are not a victim," I want to tell her, but we both know it is too late. You become a victim once you call it rape.

The morning after

At the consulting firm where I work, office romance is officially against the rules but common nonetheless. One of my colleagues—I'll call him Rick—approaches me after dinner on the final night of an off-site conference in Arizona. He invites me to skip the party and go out for a drink with him instead. He is a few years older than I am and more senior in the firm, but I don't work with him directly, and he is not my boss. He is single and athletic and not bad-looking and has a reputation for being really smart. I say yes.

The Sonoran Desert opens up beyond the irrigated

grounds of our hotel, a bleak expanse of sand and scrub grass cooling beneath the setting sun. We go to a bar on the outskirts of Scottsdale, a converted bunkhouse with a row of dusty Harleys parked out front. We settle at a picnic table, and Rick fetches himself a nonalcoholic beer and me an Amstel Light. He is fun to talk with, and I like his blue eyes and his smile. The possibility, even the likelihood, of sex flares between us like the distant heat lightning forking over the ridge of the McDowells.

I go back with Rick to his hotel room of my own free will. I am not drunk. I let him take off my clothes and lead me to the bed, filled with the strange attraction of a stranger's body touching mine. We enter such situations with certain expectations. We expect intelligent people to behave intelligently, colleagues to behave collegially, people with whom we have a lot in common to think the way we think. So when I ask him if he has a condom, I don't expect him to laugh and say, "Oh, I don't do condoms." I don't expect that he won't stop. We are two bodies in motion, and momentum exerts its force. My mind whirls, but no words come out. Very quickly, it is over. He sighs and rolls away.

I phone my doctor the next day and ask for the morning-after pill. (There is no such thing yet as over-the-counter Plan B.) I hear only what I take for disapproval in her voice as she gives me instructions, her tone clinical and clipped. I don't remember if she asks me about what happened. I'm sure she doesn't use the word *consent*. Anyway, I consented, didn't I? I could have said no, could have tried to stop him, but I did not.

I fill the prescription, swallow the pills, and for the next twenty-four hours, I throw up. I don't talk to Rick. I tell my friends I must have caught a stomach bug. The wretchedness of my secret feels like the punishment I deserve.

What is it about no means no

Jury duty, Salt Lake City, 2004. At the courthouse, people wait in rows of plastic chairs, mumbling into cell phones, as a film plays overhead about the civic importance and personal rewards of jury service. Finally, a few of us are called up to the courtroom for the voir dire. We stand in turn and answer questions printed on a laminated sheet. One of the questions is what kinds of things we read. A number of people say "only religious material." I'm an East Coast liberal, working toward an English Ph.D. I tell them: *The New Yorker*, literary fiction, Derrida. I'm thinking that I'll be dismissed.

After the questioning, the judge informs us that the criminal trial we're being selected for is a rape case. The defendant, who is married to the victim, is being tried on five counts of rape. The judge asks if anyone feels they cannot be objective in this kind of case. She asks if anyone has a problem with the concept that the defendant is innocent until proven guilty. Several people raise their hands and are excused. I'm in.

Spousal rape has been against the law in Utah, as in most states, since 1991, but the concept is still not so easy to digest. The couple in this case are young and poor and have two small kids. She works in a gas-station convenience store. He is out of work. We're told they fight over childcare and who gets to use the car. We watch a video of him being interrogated by a detective who appears to be coercing him to confess. We watch as the wife takes the stand and starts to cry, her waist-length brown hair hanging in her face, as she says she loves her husband, has always loved him, loves him still.

We understand that the law says you don't have to kick and scream or struggle for an unwanted sexual act to be considered rape. That you don't have to be physically threatened or forcibly pinned down. That you have to be capable of consent, and that you can withdraw that consent at any point. That rape is not the victim's fault. We understand all this, and yet. Listening to the testimony, we wrestle with the fact that this man did not use force, that his wife did not fight back. We sit around the table in the jury room and argue for hours, conflicted and confused.

"What bothers me is that she didn't *do* anything to stop him."

"Come on, what could she have done? She said she knew she *couldn't* stop him no matter what she did."

"She told him, 'Stop, you'll wake the kids.'"

"But was she like, 'Oh, we really should stop, honey,' or like, 'You need to stop right this minute?' How can you tell?"

"Look, it's not as if he hurt her. Bad sex isn't a crime."

"It doesn't make any difference whether or not he hurt her. She didn't want to do it. That's her right."

"Haven't we all done things we didn't want to do? That's called life."

"She got up there on the stand and said she loves him."

In the end, we can't agree to call it rape. They're both young and foolish, we rationalize. None of us wants to be responsible for ruining a young man's life.

After we deliver our not-guilty verdict, the prosecutor comes storming back. She is furious, her red hair ablaze.

She says, "What is it about 'no means no' that you all don't understand?"

Antipodes

Traveling in New Zealand, I strike up a conversation with an American in a Queenstown café. He's thirty-something, my age as well, a high school science teacher who, like me, has taken a leave of absence from work. His accent is appealingly familiar. He seems like any number of the fellow travelers I've met while on the road alone: friendly, companionable, polite. After we finish eating, he invites me to walk back with him to his hostel to watch a movie on the common room TV. It's a pleasant, early autumn evening—March in the antipodes—and I have nothing else to do, so I agree. We meander across town, chatting about Wanaka and the Milford Sound, our hikes along the Franz Joseph Glacier, the sea-eroded rocks at Hokitika, the seals basking on the beach at Jackson Bay.

At the hostel, the common room is deserted, and nothing good is playing on TV. I look around for the proprietor of the hostel, other guests, but there's no one else in sight. The fluorescent lights buzz overhead. Sitting beside him on the couch as he clicks through the channels, I feel the energy between us shift. After a bit, he puts his arm around me and pulls me to him. He tries to kiss me, but I shake my head, pull back. "I'm sorry," I say, feeling like a jerk. I didn't mean to lead him on. It really didn't occur to me that this is what he had in mind.

He stiffens, but instead of backing off, he presses closer, fumbling with the zipper of his pants with one hand, pushing my head down with the other, angling his pelvis toward my face. He does not hurt me, but there is nothing but aggression in his actions. For a moment, I consider giving in. It's just a blow job he is after, after all. But instead I pull free, stand up. His anger radiates toward me, hard and petulant as a child's, only he is no child.

"I'd better go," I say.

He says, "You fucking bitch."

I leave him sitting on the couch. Outside, in the darkness, fear catches me by the throat. It is quite a long distance back to where I'm staying, and I'm not sure I know the way. I walk as quickly as I can without running, scanning the dark streets for a taxi, for attackers, my room keys threaded through my fingers, adrenaline vibrating through my limbs. I am less angry with him than with myself. I thought I knew how to take care of myself, but I fucked up.

In my journal, I write only: *Met F. at dinner. Took a walk back to his hostel.* I edit out the details but not the shame, which lingers, even after all these years.

Rape is rape

Rape happens behind closed doors, between the sheets, in locker rooms, in prisons, in churches, in refugee camps, in dorms, in back alleys, in $3,000-per-night luxury hotel suites. It happens between the powerful and the weak, between men and women, men and boys, women and women, women and boys, husbands and wives, adults and children, strangers and lovers, between ordinary people like you and me. You might say you're just having a little fun, horsing around, hooking up. Sometimes there's a knife or a gun. Sometimes there's a kiss. It isn't so easy to tell lie from truth, intention from mistake.

After a Toronto cop tells a group of college women that they shouldn't dress provocatively if they don't want to get raped, women around the world take to the streets dressed in bras and camisoles and fishnet tights, the word *SLUT* scrawled in Sharpie across their bare arms and backs. Bloggers rail against rape culture. Activists wage campaigns for better information and awareness, trumpeting the slogan "Rape is rape." All this talk gives me a bit of hope. I'd like to think my children will grow up to a world where girls are not attacked at gunpoint in their homes or dorms or taken advantage of when drunk, where threats or accusations of rape are not used to gain political advantage, where women can express their sexuality without being shamed as sluts, where men and women understand that no means no and yes means yes. But I'm not so sure.

Maybe anatomy is destiny; maybe Freud was right. The language of desire is the language of violence, after all. Sexy women are knockouts, bombshells, stunning, dressed to kill, femmes fatales. Love is an abduction: Your heart is stolen. You're smitten, hooked, swept off your feet. Cupid's weapon is an arrow. His mouth's a bow. Sex and violence, violence and sex, twine together in a lover's knot that cannot be undone.

GHOST VARIATIONS

No one will learn anything about me from my *letters.*
—Johannes Brahms

Thema

We woke at the same moment, our hearts twanging
in our chests. There was a suffocating disturbance in the
darkness, a thrum like beating wings. I've never believed
in apparitions, visitations, angels, ghosts—and yet I felt
it. We both did. A strange, unreasonable thing. B's body
quivered like an open string, tuned to the resonance of
correspondences and signs. He knew there were things out
there that you could feel but couldn't see.

Out the window, now, the trees are flailing in the wind.
A branch scrapes against the house; acorns pelt the roof. The
sky is blackish orange, as if the hills were burning, although
it's just the city's distant tungsten haze. Wind and air are also
felt but unseen things. Music too.

Listen: to the creaking trees and rushing wind and
above it all the music, those aching F-sharp minor sonorities,
calling out your name. Somehow I thought that if I just
listened long enough, I would—

Var. 1

An impossible task, to conjure a spirit from the dead.
There's so little to go on—letters, hearsay, speculation,
a portrait sketch, a sheaf of scores. Fragments, mirrors,
ectoplasm, smoke.

A photograph: Johannes Brahms at twenty-one. Blond
hair falling to the shoulders, a high forehead, a widow's peak.

White-blond brows and lashes, light-blue eyes. One hand tucked into his coat like Goethe's Young Werther or Napoleon. His cheeks still beardless, his voice still high, they said.

What is it that's so familiar about this photograph? I rummage through my desk, searching for that other photograph, that other B. And there it is: the same blond hair swept back from a high forehead, the same blue gaze and slightly stubborn chin. The resemblance is uncanny. Except for the frock coat and sentimental pose, they could be twins. Doppelgängers. Brahms would have liked that. In those early days, he signed his compositions in the name of a fictional double, *Johannes Kreisler Jr.*, a character from E. T. A. Hoffmann's tales. The divided self refracts.

The photographer has captured B beside a wooden statue—a man's body with a horse's head. It's an avatar of Vishnu, Hayagriva, worshipped for rescuing the sacred Vedas from the demons. In Hinduism, Hayagriva represents the triumph of knowledge over evil, although the statue held a different significance for B. He took the horse's head as a reminder not to speak of what he knew—things the rest of us were not yet prepared to hear.

I speak in my music, Brahms once wrote. Better to weave a story out of eighth notes and appoggiaturas, chords and quavers, counterpoint. Theme and variations—yes.

Var. 2

Düsseldorf, September 1853. Brahms is standing before the blue doors of Bilker Straße 1032, Schumann's house. He adjusts his rucksack, shakes back his hair, stringy after a week of tramping along the Rhine. His boots are muddy, perhaps, his jacket not so very clean. A carriage clatters past along the cobblestones. In the distance, the afternoon bells of St. Lambertus begin to chime. He raises his hand to knock. He will not go back with nothing to show for his trip. He will not return unrecognized to philistine Hamburg, where the sky hangs gray as a dishrag over the North Sea docks. He will not be like his father, buffoonish in his Bürgerwehr plumed cap, playing the bugle in a pavilion in the park. Inside him the tritone clangs, the devil's own diminished fifth. *Mit meinem in c-ges gestimmten Herzen*: "my C–G-flat-tuned heart."

Here is Brahms at twenty, then, stepping across the Schumanns' threshold, Robert bending to embrace him, Clara smiling at her husband's side. The boy will play for them his C-major sonata, his F-sharp minor sonata, his scherzo in E flat. *Visit from Brahms (a genius)*, Schumann will note afterward in his diary. He touches Brahms on the shoulder, a king dubbing a commoner a knight. His dressing gown flaps in the breeze. His eyes are a little wild, even then. *You and I understand each other*, he says. Schumann is quoting E. T. A. Hoffmann's antihero, the Kapellmeister Kreisler speaking to Johannes Kreisler Jr., his apprentice, his double, his protégé: *Ah, my dear Johannes, who knows you better than I do, who has so deeply looked into you, nay, has looked out from inside you?* Did Schumann know the boy had signed the scores of the pieces he just performed *Johannes Kreisler Jr.* and not Johannes Brahms?

Kreis means "circle" in German. Everything comes full circle in the end. There's no such thing as coincidence, B always said. Whenever he said that, I never knew what to think.

Var. 3

Doubles, circles, correspondences: Everywhere you look you find those old Romantic conceits. Nobody goes in for it anymore, all that mooning over nature and ancient ruins, but I'm attracted to it all the same, the privileging of emotion over reason, the notion of an excess of feeling beyond what you can rationally understand.

They doubled and circled each other in their music, Robert and Clara Schumann, and Johannes Brahms. Wove into their compositions layers of quotations, echoes, allusions to one another's works. For her husband's forty-third birthday in 1853, Clara wrote a set of variations on a theme from the first Albumblatt from Robert's *Bunte Blätter* variations. In 1854 Brahms wrote for Clara a set of sixteen variations on the same theme, *Variations on a Theme by Robert Schumann,* opus 9. Brahms's tenth variation quotes Clara's seventh variation in which she quotes her own *Romance,* a piece she wrote for Robert when she was just thirteen. Schumann wrote his *Impromptus* (another set of variations) in response, and Brahms's fifteenth variation quotes that piece as well. Variations on variations on variations. An infinite regression. A palimpsest.

It's a double love story, of course: the famous romance of Robert Schumann and the child prodigy Clara Wieck; the perhaps even more famous romance of Clara Schumann and Johannes Brahms. If *romance* is the word. If there *are* words to describe the complicated yearning of a young man for an older woman, of a lonely woman for a lover, of a budding composer for a famous pianist, of an artist for a muse.

I put the recording of Brahms's opus 9 variations on the stereo. *Short Variations on a Theme by Him, for Her,* he scribbled on the autograph of the score. There's a whisper of static, a faint echo as the piano sounds. The theme is deceptively simple: a progression of F-sharp minor harmonies descending C#–B–A–G#–A to "spell" Clara's name. The chords modulate from minor to major and back to minor, building to an intense sforzando cry. The harmonic voices mingle and then fade, as lovers' voices do. It's not so easy to distinguish art from love.

Var. 4

The problem of imagining another life is a problem of time. Ghosts, by definition, make present what is past. But we see right through them to the other side.

They were Germans born before the unification of Germany, before electricity and automobiles and recorded music and the two world wars, before Einstein and Schoenberg and Hitler and Freud, before the entire century that we've already left behind. A time of crinolines and horse-drawn carriages and frock coats and quill pens and candlelight, although by the 1850s things were already changing—steam engines and petroleum and gunpowder grinding mankind toward the threshold of modern times. They considered themselves moderns, even then.

In the year 1854—the year Johannes Brahms composes the opus 9 variations and falls in love with another man's wife—Oscar Wilde, Arthur Rimbaud, John Philip Sousa, Thomas Watson, and Alfred Krupp are born; Vincent Van Gogh and Cecil Rhodes turn one; Commodore Perry forces Japan to open its ports to Western trade; France and England declare war on Russia; Dickens serializes *Hard Times*; Harriet Tubman sends the first slaves along the Underground Railroad; Walt Whitman works on *Leaves of Grass*; Florence Nightingale departs for the Crimea; the Suez Canal is inaugurated; Nadar makes his first daguerreotypes; Thoreau publishes *Walden* and Tennyson "The Charge of the Light Brigade"; Chopin is dead and George Sand is writing her memoirs; Berlioz's oratorio *The Infant Christ* premiers, along with Liszt's *Preludes*. It has been nearly one hundred years since Mozart's birth, twenty-seven years since Beethoven died.

A bust of Beethoven looks down on Brahms from its place of honor on a shelf in the Schumanns' music room. Even in cold marble, you can feel the energy in that wild hair, that craggy brow. Brahms feels Beethoven's gaze as a reproach.

Too late, those eyes say. It's all been done before.

B was born belatedly as well. Mysticism, these days, is nothing but pathology, visions a function of the chemistry of the brain. The age of the prophets long ago gone past.

Var. 5

What I remember. B improvising at the piano, his fingers mirrored in the glossy black. A cascade of notes, a thread of melody. He finishes, slides over on the bench, and turns to me. "Now you play," he says, but despite all my years of piano lessons, I cannot. I'm as stiff as the horse-headed god standing mute behind me on his pedestal, hands pressed to his wooden sides. I'd like to say there's something trapped inside me—a flutter-spark of inspiration beating like a tiny wing—but I feel nothing but pulp and sawdust, an unyielding whorl.

I wrote music as a child: a canon, a sonatina, a trio for piano and strings. The trio won a prize; professional musicians performed it at a children's concert. My grandparents broadcast the recording over the PA system in their factory. I remember twisting with embarrassment as the reels of tape spun around like the self-destructing instructions at the start of *Mission Impossible*. Piped over the speakers, the music sounded nothing like the sound I'd heard inside my head.

Now I sit down at the piano and sight-read Brahms's opus 9 variations. I trace the melody among the interwoven voices, parsing the sharps and double sharps and flats, fumbling through the turbulent arpeggios and octaves, the densely clustered chords. I stretch my fingers across the keys where Brahms once stretched his much broader span. I can't come close to playing the music the way he intended it to be played.

On the autograph of the score, Brahms extended the double bars on eleven of the sixteen variations to form the initials *Kr* for *Kreisler*, *B* for *Brahms*. The more flamboyant, fantastical variations belong to Kreisler; the calmer, more lyrical ones to Brahms. To Clara he wrote, *I often argue with myself, which means that Kreisler and Brahms are struggling . . . both are utterly confused, and neither knows what he wants.* The theme-and-variation form pulls him between the poles of liberation and constraint, criticism and homage. Wild Kreisler and dutiful Brahms wrestle within his heart. I know: they wrestle in my heart as well.

Var. 6

The 1850s are the heyday of spiritualism. Ever since the weird sisters Katie and Margaret Fox summoned the spirit of a murdered peddler buried beneath their Hydesville, New York, house, conjuring the otherworldly has been all the rage. Mesmerized mediums in darkened parlors usher forth the dead. The spirits communicate through an obscure Morse code of knocks and taps. Magnetic forces ripple like strange tides through the psychics' bodies, guiding quivering pens to spell out esoteric codes.

Séances catch on in Europe in 1853. English ladies in high-necked gowns rest gloved fingers on the edges of fringed cloth-covered tea tables, holding their breath. If the energy is right, the table will begin to turn; spinning faster and faster, it may even rise into the air. In Düsseldorf, Robert Schumann conducts "magnetic experiments" with friends and family around the little table in his music room. The spirits rap and moan. The polished walnut whirls. *One is surrounded with miracles!* Schumann writes to his friend Hiller. He grows animated on séance days, jovial and flushed. The spirits beat the opening rhythm of Beethoven's Fifth Symphony; they channel the energies of Schubert and Mozart.

Photographs are a kind of spirit too—traces of ghostly light recovered from the past like the belated light of stars.

According to the photographer Nadar, Balzac dreaded being photographed, believing that *every body in its natural state was made up of a series of ghostly images superimposed in layers to infinity, wrapped in infinitesimal films* that the daguerreotype would somehow seize hold of, detach, use up. Eventually William Mumler will make the photograph into a literal "medium" for channeling the spirit world, his plates revealing images of ectoplasmic figures hovering behind his subjects' heads. Desire made manifest in silver iodide and mercury. Of course, he turns out to be a fraud.

Here are those photographs: black-and-white portraits of Robert and Clara Schumann and Johannes Brahms. B and his wooden horse. The photographs tell me . . . nothing. Only that once a person composed himself before the camera's voyeuristic eye. And what is a composition but a pose?

Var. 7

The past is static, two-dimensional, monotones of black and white and gray. I want more—I want to smell the horse dung clumped along the cobblestones, the musty horsehair-stuffed upholstery, the rosin dust and candle wax and days-old ashes in the grate, the milk turned sour in the milking can, the sweat-stained armpits of a linen shirt. I want to taste their cheap red wine, inhale the smoke of their cigars, Joachim and Dietrich and Grimm and Brahms, as they gather, laughing, in the Hofgarten café at night. I want to feel the breeze as Brahms chases the Schumann children through the bushes in the Gräfenberg, turning somersaults on the muddy ground. I want to smell the damp grass of the embankment where he lies beside his buddy Dietrich, watching the moon rise above the Rhine. I want to hear the children gasp as he performs handstands on the banister of the front-hall stairs. I want to hear the cat yowling in the alley, the nursemaid calling to the children, the muffled sound of one of Clara's pupils running through her scales. I want to taste the torte the cook bakes for Brahms when he turns twenty-one. The children cluster around the piano, singing him a song. Clara, eight months pregnant with her seventh child, plays for him the variations she wrote for Robert's birthday the year before. Her glossy brown hair is parted in the middle, looped in braids over her ears; she wears a white-lace collar pinned around her neck. She presses a handkerchief to her lips. Oh, this boy with his quivering intensity, his long fine fingers, his too-blue gaze! Such energy! Sometimes it sounds as if there are two people at the piano when it's just him alone. When he looks at her, she feels as if she has been cast in gold.

Var. 8

What I remember. A dinner party at B's loft downtown. Beautiful people, pulsing music, B's canvases leaning against the walls. The rapturous chocolate cake in which someone suddenly sees a vision of the Black Madonna and we burst spontaneously into song—the "Hallelujah Chorus"—our arms wrapped around one another's shoulders, swaying in the candlelight. I assume they've all been friends forever, only to discover that nearly all of them met B for the first time just the night before. We flutter like dazzled moths around his flame.

My other friends wear suits to work, are busy getting married, making money, buying houses in the suburbs, having kids. B is a too-bright light shining in my eyes. In the bloom of his radiance, I am overexposed. He holds out his hand and I step onto the wire. "Trust me," he says. Behind him are the paintings, planes of color and whirl. They are puzzle pieces, he says, hinting at a story that can't be told in words. He talks instead about geometry, cosmology, systems of signs. The word *crazy* buzzes at the edges of my brain. I swat it away and let him reel me in. In my peripheral vision: a man's body with a horse's head.

Late at night, I forget B's warnings and stand up in the dark and whack my forehead hard on the low beam of the sleeping loft in his apartment, giving myself a black bruised ring beneath one eye. He has marked me, then.

Var. 9

The end is already visible at the beginning, if only you know how to read the signs. A snake biting its tail.

Schumann is only forty-three, but you can see it leaching out of him, the will to live, if only you know to look for it, like a bruise spreading outward on a rotting pear. His skin is jaundiced from laudanum or arsenic, his pupils dilated, his hair greasy and limp. His sensualist's lips are pursed as if he has just tasted something sour. Already on the day of Brahms's first visit, Clara has written in her diary: *I am more discouraged than I can possibly say.* For some time Schumann has been hearing voices. Angels circle, calling to him in *exquisite, unbearable harmonies,* or a low and droning A. He has become Hoffmann's mad Kapellmeister Kreisler, shadowed by a guttered candle, modulating obsessively from key to key. *The notes come to life and flutter and dance around me,* Kreisler cries, *electric sparks flying through my fingertips into the keys!* And yet Kreisler, so inspired, cannot write. A ghastly red-eyed apparition sends him running for the silent sanctuary of the Benedictine monks. Schumann, likewise, is undone by dissonance and harmony. Over the years, there have been other highs of divine inspiration, flat spells of deep despair. The darkness visible, closing in. Manic depression, we might call it now, or schizophrenia. It is difficult to tell.

I discover the bottles of lithium and Prozac in B's medicine cabinet not long after we first meet. I am snooping, I admit. I cup the orange prescription bottles in my palm and feel the floor tip beneath my feet. How impossible it is to know another person! Brahms, too, prowled behind closed doors—searched Schumann's papers, letters, diaries, notes, and scores. *Almost the whole day I sit in Bilker Straße 1032 on the second floor,* he writes to Clara. *I must search through everything!* He's still too young, perhaps, to understand that it may be better not to know. Later he learns to leave no trace. He asks for his letters back and burns them, tells Clara to do the same.

Less than six months after Brahms arrives in Düsseldorf, Schumann is in torment, the world reverberating with hallucinated tones. He can't sleep, can't think; he paces and screams and tears his hair. Clara sits with him in the dark. Inside her she feels the newest baby's flutter kick. At last Schumann picks up his quill. He writes five variations on the angels' deadly theme: *Ghost Variations.* Clara recognizes the melody from the slow movement of Schumann's own Violin Concerto in D minor, written earlier that year. At dawn she leaves him at his desk, copying out the score. When she returns, he's gone.

Which red-eyed specter sends him running along the Bilker Straße that February morning, barefoot in the freezing rain? The pontoon bridge stretches long and low across the gun-gray water of the Rhine. Schumann pushes past the toll collector, shoves his scarf into the man's baffled hands, and runs headlong onto the span, his heart a tocsin in his chest, his tongue thick in his throat. The angels circle him like rays of light. He stops midway across, gasping, the wind stronger there and cold, his cheeks on fire, his feet gone numb. He ducks beneath the rail. He looks down onto the ice-skimmed river, wind-whipped into chop. Balances on the edge.

The gold of it catches his eye then. He wrenches the wedding band from his finger—the old injured third finger of his right hand. *Clärchen,* he has written, *do the same with yours.* Deep in the muddy silt, the rings will reunite. He hurls the ring into the Rhine. It drops as if in suspended motion, a glinting circle in the winter light, falling like a sigh. He watches it disappear, then steps off into air.

Var. 10

Schumann's suicide attempt sets Brahms's bright new world atilt. Schumann, having been fished out of the river by a passing trawler, is sent off to an asylum in Endenich, near Bonn, where he's permitted to see no one, not even his wife. Brahms and his young musician friends—Joachim, Dietrich, Grimm—gather around Clara that spring and summer of 1854, trying to raise her spirits as she waits for her baby to be born. They make music in the evenings after the children have been put to bed, playing Hungarian folk tunes, Clementi, Schubert, Weber, all of Schumann's songs. They run through Brahms's new two-piano sonata, his piano trio in B. But nothing can drown out the ostinato of Clara's weeping, the pedal point of calamity.

Brahms is homesick. He's flat broke; he's published nothing yet. *A young eagle*, Schumann called him, and he longs for fame, but without his mentor, he cannot hope to fly. He reworks his first two piano sonatas, composes two trios and a quartet. He tries to write a piano concerto and fails. He works on small pieces instead: the opus 9 variations, the Four Ballades. He dreams of a nightingale impaling itself upon a thorn. He frescoes the walls of his rented rooms with Madonna faces and demon heads.

In August, Clara leaves Düsseldorf for the seaside, and Brahms heads to the Schwarzwald, seeking inspiration in the romantic vistas of the Rhine. It's all there: the red-roofed houses, knobby spires, terraced vineyards, stately chestnuts, the flowing Neckar, and, beyond, the densely wooded hills. But the misty views and castle ruins do not feel picturesque. In his cheap room at the inn, the candle sputters and drips. He can't stand the trilling in his gut; he's not himself at all. He dips his nib into the pot of ink. His friend Joachim is right: he's like Young Werther, Goethe's tragic hero, tramping moodily about in nature, yearning for another man's wife. He can see himself in Werther's blue swallowtail jacket and yellow waistcoat, holding a pistol to his head. He is a fool.

He cuts his holiday short and hurries back to Düsseldorf, where he writes letter after letter to Clara, longing for her return. He travels to Endenich to visit Schumann in the asylum, but he is permitted only to peer from behind a curtained window as the older man strolls in the gardens. Schumann puffs on his pipe, flutters a cotton handkerchief in one hand. He bends to inspect the roses through his lorgnette, straightens, walks on. From a distance, he looks much the same as ever, but he is not the same, not better, not at all. He's still tormented by hallucinated tones and voices. He speaks wildly, screams in his sleep. The doctor takes Brahms aside. *Tell Frau Schumann please that she must not delude herself with hopes of an early recovery.* Hope dangles on a fraying thread.

Back in Düsseldorf, Brahms gives the Schumann children piano lessons. He teaches the older girls to play selections from Robert's *Pictures from the East.* He manages to compose two additional variations on the Schumann theme, numbers 10 and 11. He writes to Joachim: *Through one of them Clara speaks!* Even in her absence, her fragrance lingers in the air. He makes a note in the margin of the tenth variation: *Rose and heliotrope smelled sweet.*

He writes: *I love her and am under her spell . . . I think I can no longer love an unmarried girl . . . at least, I have quite forgotten about them. They only promise heaven while Clara shows it revealed . . . .*

Writes: *I often have to restrain myself forcibly from just quietly putting my arms around her . . . . It seems so natural . . .*

And to Clara, he writes: *You have no idea how indispensable your presence is for me, you have not the remotest conception . . . . I can no longer exist without you . . . . Please go on loving me as I shall go on loving you always and forever.*

He presses a camellia blossom into the letter's fold. Uses for the first time the intimate second person pronoun, *du.*

Var. 11

A famous pianist gives a concert at the college where I teach. I slide into a seat up front. A Steinway concert grand occupies center stage, its ebony lid raised like a curving wing. The program begins with Brahms's Ballades. The pianist takes the microphone before he plays. "Imagine Brahms at twenty-one," he says, "blond and beardless, a boy in love. Imagine the hazy darkness of a summer garden, a nightingale's low trill."

Listen: to the dark D-minor landscape of octaves and open fifths, to the triplets roiling like the sea, to the voices rising and falling, the minor-mode digressions that ache like yearning. Remember: There are many kinds of love. What kind of love was theirs? We turn and turn the puzzle pieces, but they will not fit. Why is it so hard to picture? Because she is thirty-four and married and a mother, and he's just turned twenty-one? Because they're buttoned-up Victorians bound by the moral strictures of the church? Because all we have to go on are a handful of ink-scrawled letters with a surplus of meaning tucked between the lines? Because sex only exists in the present tense, unfolding in real time?

At home, I pull out the sheet music of the first Ballade. The epigraph is a reference to "Edward," an old Scottish poem. It tells the story of a prince who kills his father for his mother's love:

> *Why dois your brand sae drap wi bluid*
> *Edward, Edward?*
> *Why dois your brand sae drap wi bluid*
> *And why sae sad gang ye O?*

You can hear it in the music: the octave bell-tones tolling, the triplets struggling against duplets, the anguished chromatic rise. Edward's terrible last words to his mother hang in the diabolic dissonance of A-flat and D: *The curse of hell frae me shall ye beir/Sic counseils ye gave to me O.* It's hard not to cast

Robert as the murdered patriarch, Clara as the beguiling queen, poor old Oedipal Johannes as the guilt-wracked heir.

And yet music shouldn't depend on any story. Brahms famously insisted upon that. He understood that meaning can't be pinned in place like a butterfly's bright wings. That meaning, in music as in poetry, transcends words. *Negative Capability*, Keats called it, *when a man is capable of being in uncertainties, Mysteries, doubts, without any irritable reaching after fact & reason . . . .*

I felt something, I tell you, that night in the suffocating dark with B. An uncertainty, a mystery, a doubt. Why can't I just let it be?

Var. 12

One of B's paintings is of a giant swing, the kind you find at old-fashioned amusement parks. The swing tilts at a crazy angle, the riders soaring outward in a rising arc. In the foreground, the swing's high crown is decorated with intricate jewel tones and gold leaf, ornate as an illuminated manuscript or a Persian rug. The riders, by contrast, are rough dabs of blue and yellow paint flung against a deep magenta ground. The impression is one of vertigo and swirl. If you look closely, you'll see that chains on one of the swings have snapped, sending the rider—clutching what looks like a briefcase, or an enormous book—tumbling toward a black abyss.

Despite the horse-headed Hayagriva's warning, B talks. He tells me a story of breakdown and exorcism, despair and revelation, of esoteric messages he's been learning to decode. He is sketching, stretching canvases on six-foot frames, planning a new series of paintings: another sort of variations on a theme. He holds out his thumb at arm's length, squints at it through one eye, calculates the angle of perspective, gauges the direction of the light. Does he even see me there,

my head level with his thumb? The loft reeks of paint and
turpentine; the chairs are draped in drop cloths, dirty dishes
piled in the sink. He takes off his watch, does not go to work.
In the bathroom, I glance at the bottles of his pills. Is he
brilliant or mad? Or both? Do I love him? I don't know what
to think.

In the washed light of the early summer morning,
I walk back to my apartment across town. The breeze is
nudging wisps of shredded cloud across the Lower Manhattan
sky. Korean grocers are cranking up their metal awnings,
setting out crates of vegetables and fruit. At home I pull on
pantyhose, a blouse and suit. I grab my briefcase and take a
cab uptown to work. And as I turn to the charts and graphs
and sentences in the blue-covered report it is my job to write,
I hear it: a voice as seductive as a lover's; a droning, low,
repeated B. It's the voice of that rider falling from his swing,
tumbling like one of Milton's angels through the charged
vermillion air. Let go, it says. Be free.

Var. 13

Christmas 1854. Clara sends Brahms's opus 9 variations
to Robert as a present, along with a portrait sketch of Brahms.
She has not been permitted to see her husband for nearly
an entire year. He has not asked for her, has not spoken her
name. He has never met his infant son. After Christmas,
Brahms moves into the Schumanns' house, where he will
live through 1855 and into the summer of 1856. By then,
Schumann will be dead.

Maybe Clara offers him the room as a gift, a respite
from debt, a space in which to write. Maybe she feels better
knowing he'll be there, helping the nursemaid Bertha with
the children while she's away on concert tour for weeks.
Maybe she sees him as a sort of eldest son; after all, he's only
eight years older than her eldest daughter, Marie. And maybe

that is how he sees himself—as an adopted child, an heir. Or maybe he sees himself as the man of the family, instead, filling Schumann's too-big, abandoned shoes. Surely it is Clara he imagines as his lover, soulmate, muse, wife. Maybe she sees it that way, too.

To the seven Schumann children, Brahms becomes father, mother, brother, uncle, gymnastics instructor, music teacher, babysitter, tutor, nurse. He tussles with the boys, bribing them to learn the alphabet with sugar lumps and sweets. He joins the girls for tea. He lets little Ludwig crawl into his bed in the middle of the night. He takes care of them when they're sick, calms their fears, oversees the nanny and the cook. He writes Clara letter after letter when she's away, her portrait medallion propped before him on her desk. He follows the glowing reviews of her recitals in the newspaper. He ignores the letters from his mother: *You are on the wrong track—you will amount to absolutely nothing.* They jangle in his pocket like a broken string.

In July 1855 he returns to the Rhineland for a five-day holiday, but this time he is not alone. This time, the landscape is infused with beauty. He sits with Clara on a bench overlooking the Lorelei rock, the Rhine flowing below. The fairy-tale turrets of Burg Katz soar against the cloud-streaked sky. The slate cliffs of Sankt Goarshausen glow pink in the evening sun. At this bend in the river, legend has it, love-struck fishermen ran aground, bewitched by the siren Lorelei's song. Perhaps his fingers brush against Clara's then, close around them, folding them into his own. She has large, strong hands, a virtuoso's fingers, finely formed and long. Perhaps he is thinking of E. T. A. Hoffmann again, of the scene where Kreisler dreams of a rock whose *veins blossomed into dark carnations whose fragrance rose almost visibly in bright, sounding rays,* which then condensed *into the figure of a beautiful woman . . . the form of divine, delightful music.*

And Clara? She feels the blood pulse beneath the pale

skin of his hands, pumping through the muscle of his heart. *He draws in great breaths of nature*, she writes in her diary, *and one grows young with him*. Desire roils like a chromatic scale. Hangs in the air like a diminished fifth, dissonant, unresolved.

Just that once, B and I went away together to the country on a holiday. That was where it happened—in the suffocating darkness of an unfamiliar place—that awful pressure on our chests, that rush of beating wings. Something touched us then, an angel or a ghost. We knew it was a sign. Only I didn't know then that to each of us, it meant a different thing.

Var. 14

Variations, like infatuation, make a fetish of their theme.

The theme—the loved one—disappears. Is reconstituted as an object of desire.

From time to time I reflect on variation form, Brahms writes to Joachim in 1856. *I sometimes find that [we] . . . worry the theme. We anxiously retain the entire melody, but don't manipulate it freely. We don't really create anything new out of it; on the contrary, we only burden it. The melody thus becomes scarcely recognizable.*

To Clara he has written: *I think of you as going to the concert hall like a priestess to the altar.* Now he writes: *I shall have sometime to put you under glass or have you set in gold.* He no longer uses the intimate pronoun *du*. She's an icon on a pedestal, as rigid as a preconceived idea, and mute.

I, too, fit the contours of B's iconography, at least for a while. I looked like the green-eyed, dark-haired girl he believed it was his destiny to find. I thought I was special, but he didn't really see *me* at all. In the blue light of his gaze, I ceased to exist.

The crush crushes the image at its heart. The mirror cracks.

The summer I was thirteen, I was given the piano part of Clara Schumann's Piano Trio in G Minor at a conservatory music camp. The piece was difficult, above my level of technique, and I practiced harder than I ever had before. The veins stood out across the backs of my hands; calluses formed along my fingertips. A fan oscillated in the window of our practice room; my thighs stuck to the piano bench in the humid July heat. The voices of the strings and piano rose and fell in the green promise of that leafy summer light. I don't remember much about the boy on whom I had a crush, the first crush of those early adolescent years. What I remember now is just the music, Clara's music, the last piece she wrote, long before she met Johannes Brahms. I take it out and sit down at the piano and pick through my old part. I recognize it only now: the sound of pure yearning: turbulent, nostalgic, bittersweet.

Var. 15

It couldn't last, of course. The end was visible from the start.

B and I had no future and no past; a story such as ours could only circle, double back, repeat. Like Clara, I shouldn't have watched but did when B walked away with his arm around another girl. I wasn't surprised. I just didn't expect to feel such a jagged rip.

It was only later that B spoke to me of that night we woke together in suffocating darkness to that strange shared dream. We were sitting beneath blue pendant lights in a downtown bar. He said: "Tell me what you felt, then." I traced the letters in the condensation on my glass. Hollowness ached inside my chest. I didn't answer his question. I thought: Probably it was just claustrophobia. Probably we got disoriented in the dark. Probably we'd had too much to drink.

He tore a piece of paper from a notebook and handed it to me. He looked at me intently, his blond hair brushing his shoulders. I felt the way I had that day at the piano when he urged me to improvise and I did not play. But I took the paper that he offered. I folded it and put it in my bag. "Write about it," he said. Eventually, I did.

Var. 16

In Düsseldorf, hope evaporates in the stifling August heat. *I find I cannot compose*, Brahms writes. Six years will pass before he publishes another piece. He sprawls unhappily on the couch in Clara's sitting room, writing her yet another letter, chewing an unlit cigar. He's thinking about Mozart, who'd go off to some Salzburg café and dash off a new piece, just like that. *Now* that *was a Man!*

He has set aside the Hoffmann, all that romantic Sturm und Drang. Kreisler is receding, fading away; Brahms has won. The opus 9 variations are the last composition he'll sign as *Kreisler Jr.*, his youthful alter ego's name. Somewhere, in those static months of waiting, he has made his choice. He will never marry or have children. Over the years, he will metamorphose into the white-bearded figure we think of when we think of Brahms, puffed out in a black coat and buttoned vest, encircled in smoke from a cigar. The long-haired boy with the girlish voice and pale, soft cheeks will be nothing but a long-lost ghost. He will disappear.

For months now, Schumann has been fading. He's been suffering from seizures, babbling unintelligibly, refusing to eat. The telegraph from Endenich arrives in late July 1856: *If you want to see your husband while he is still alive, hurry here immediately.* Brahms sits by Clara in the railway carriage, racing the angel of death to Bonn. The steam engine whistle shrieks; the landscape streaks past in a blur. Just the month before, he gave Schumann an atlas at his request: eighty-three maps, beautifully leather bound. Clara twists a handkerchief between her fingers. Veins as blue as rivers wind over the metacarpals of her hands. Ahead of them, Schumann lies dying, or already dead. No map can guide him through the place where he is headed now.

Listen: to the sixteenth and final variation of the opus 9 variations. *Ziemlich langsam, pianissimo.* The melody fractured across a line of octaves in the bass.

Schumann is still alive, though barely, when they arrive at Endenich. For the first time in two and a half years, the doctors let Clara in. She kneels beside the bed and grasps her husband's hand. He twitches, mutters unintelligible words. The wasted skin hangs loosely on his face, revealing the lineaments of his skull. Clara dips her finger into a glass of wine and touches it to his lips. Only once does he reach for her and try to speak:

—*My*—

—*I—know*—

Listen: to the chords rising to *forte* just for one last moment, the treble and bass coming together for the first and only time, a final cry. A sustained half note. Then *piano* again, diminishing, fading away.

The windows have been thrown open to the buzzing July heat. Are Schumann's angels still circling, singing their ghostly melody? Brahms will later write a final set of variations for four hands on the angels' theme. A requiem, a dirge.

Listen: hushed octaves in the left hand, a broken F-sharp major chord. A spare, sustained sonority. Notes skipping like a dying heartbeat, fading to *pianississimo.* The last tones drop below the threshold of perception yet continue all the same, like the sympathetic vibration of an open string.

Here, too, the windows are open to the summer heat.

Dusk is falling. Birds twitter, hidden, in the trees—the whistle of a cardinal, the cooing of a dove. The fragrance of rose and heliotrope drifts on the evening breeze. I stand up from the piano and close the lid over the keys.

THE BRAHMIC EGG

1.

*Every particle in this body is continually changing; no
one has the same body for many minutes together, and yet
we think of it as the same body.*

—Swami Vivekananda

For eleven weeks, I threw up in the late afternoons,
shivered and broke out in sweats, grew tender-breasted,
bloated, round in the cheeks. My tongue swam in my mouth.
I ate grapefruit and soft-boiled eggs. I loosened my waistband,
fell asleep under my desk. Inside my body, cells collided and
combined, broke apart and formed again. I pressed my cheek
to the carpet and shut my eyes against the light. I listened to
my blood.

The body keeps its secrets. I was dumb, a dupe. We
moved through space together, my body and I, but I knew
nothing. I slept on my left side, knees curled to chest. I had
orgasms in my dreams. Outside my bedroom window, the
mountains' flanks stretched out in the spring light, brown as
skin with patches of soft green. At night, the moon slid past
the edge of the skylight above my bed, a watchful eye. The
body closes like an envelope, a *kosha*, like the shell membrane
of an egg. I felt a pulling inside my abdomen, like loose skin
stretching tight. I sat cross-legged on the floor with my hands
palm-up on my knees. I pressed the tip of my tongue against
my teeth, closed my eyes, and focused on my brow point, the
third eye. A black planet pulsed and radiated behind my lids.
I tried to sense the vibration of the universe, the visible sound
of *Om*.

2.

When you see the unborn, uncreated, unconditioned, you are liberated from everything.

—Gautama Siddhartha

Sometimes there is blood but not always. Sometimes there is no sign at all. Sometimes there is just a brown smudge like a trace of mud on the back of your hand, which is what happened to me. It might have meant nothing, but when I saw it, I knew. It came to me that the flooding queasiness, the drapery of fatigue, the metallic taste in my mouth, had all disappeared, as if they had seeped through a pinhole too small to perceive, leaving behind the familiar self I'd been longing for all those weeks, like a residue of ash. I didn't wake my husband. I lay there next to him in the dark, listening to him breathe.

The next morning, I lay on a crinkling paper-covered examination table and stared at the fluorescent lights. The nurse-midwife squirted jelly on my stomach and slid her heartbeat monitor in a slow circle around my pelvic bones. We waited for the rapid woof-woof-woof of a seed-sized heart but heard only the slower thunking of my own. "Don't worry," the nurse said, "it's probably just too soon for us to hear a heartbeat, anyway. Maybe you've miscalculated the date. Been feeling sick?" She wiped the goo off my belly with a paper towel. "Then probably everything is fine."

She sent me down to ultrasound, where I waited for an hour as a succession of couples came out of the examination room, smiling, clutching videotapes in their hands. "Congratulations," I heard the doctor say, "everything looks fine." In a small office across from where I sat, a technician prepared syringes for drawing blood. She took a latex glove

90

out of a box and blew it into a balloon for a fussy child, a bloodless hand.

The radiologist called me in. "Oh, I'm sure everything is fine," he said cheerfully. In the grainy darkness, I tried to breathe. Gray shapes formed and reformed on the monitor screen. "Here's your uterus," he said, pressing down hard with the probe. A pear-shaped outline shaded gray slid onto the screen like a misshapen moon. Then only gray. The doctor moved the probe up and around, then set it down. "I'm very sorry," he said.

I'd pictured a dead baby shaped like a seahorse, knees curled to chin, as in the intrauterine photographs shown in biology books. But there was nothing but darkness, blank and black as outer space. There was nothing there at all.

3.

This body, formed out of the five elements by the creator, is known as Brahma-anda *(the Brahmic egg). It is created for the experience of pleasure and pain.*
—The Shiva-Samhita

It was a "blighted ovum," my doctor said. It sounded like a biblical plague. I stood in her office in my raincoat, my wet umbrella in my hand, and began to cry. She came over and gave me a hug. "One in every four pregnancies spontaneously aborts," she told me. This was something I had not known. "The fetus just doesn't develop; something goes wrong, for reasons we don't know. It is not your fault." I nodded like a child and took the tissue she held out. Then she said, "The bleeding should start soon."

I called my husband from my cell phone in the car. He said, "We can try again." I called my mother when I got home. She said, "Honey, you know that these things happen for the best." My mother endured six miscarriages after she had me, one a girl born alive at nineteen weeks whom they didn't even try to save. She spent months on bed rest every time. I remember coming home from school to see her propped on pillows, knitting or reading, supine on the couch. I remember her crying a lot. Eventually she had my brother, nearly nine years after me.

My girlfriend took me shopping at the mall. I didn't know what tense to use—I've had a miscarriage, I'm having one, I'll have one soon? She simply said, "I'm sorry," which I was grateful for. I didn't fit into any regular-sized clothes, so I just sat with her as she tried on shoes, trying not to think of the stunted amniotic sac inside me, its useless placenta still pumping out hormones obliviously.

I walked through the cemetery in the Avenues, near our house, the tombstones stained gray in the spring rain. Magpies chattered and wheeled around the pines. I looked at the names: German, Swedish, Irish, an Italian, a Slav. A small section was all Chinese. No relatives of mine. Husbands and wives and children lay side by side beneath the ground. Under a sycamore, a half-sized marble headstone for a child.

Can you mourn a death when there's no body? When there never was a heart that beat? The Talmud says life begins only at twenty weeks, when movement quickens in the womb. You can't light a yahrzeit candle or say kaddish for a fetus. You can't leave a pebble on a grave.

4.

Yoni-mudra (womb-seal) is executed while seated in the siddha-asana, with eyes, ears, and nostrils closed with the ten fingers. It consists in forcing the life energy (prana) *through the six psychoenergetic centers* (chakras) *of the body.*
—Svatmarama Yogindra

I sat on the toilet and listened to the sound of blood falling into water. It fell in an alarming, steady stream, deep magenta, lumpy with glistening, liverish clots. The on-call had instructed me to watch for any fetal matter I might pass—"it looks grayish, kind of like chicken," she explained—so I took a plastic take-out container into the bathroom with me, but I didn't manage to catch anything in it but what looked like blood. I hunched forward over my knees, my hands pressed against my face, as the cramps grew more severe, like the contractions of labor. The trickle continued. No one had told me there would be so much blood.

After an hour or so, my husband opened the bathroom door a crack and peered in. "Are you okay?" he asked. "I don't know," I said. The on-call had told me to come in to the emergency room for a D&C if I thought I might be hemorrhaging. My husband handed the phone to me and I paged her again. When the phone rang, she sounded sleepy and annoyed. "I'll meet you there," she said.

I was dizzy and nauseated by the time we got to the ER, and my sweatpants were saturated with blood. The triage nurse took me right away, hooked me up to an IV and covered me with a paper sheet, then left us in the cubicle with its greenish walls and curtain pleated like an accordion. The pain was bad. My husband sat on a stool by my side and held my hand. I was glad he was there. It was past midnight, and there was a tired puffiness around his eyes. He said, "I'm sorry that you have to go through this." I said, "I don't want to have a baby." He said, "You don't have to."

5.

The shava-asana *(corpse pose) is done to reduce stress and tension. Lying on your back, let your arms and legs drop open, with the arms about 45 degrees from the sides of your body. Close your eyes. Release control of the breath, the mind and the body.*

—Hatha Yoga Manual

The on-call was a disconcertingly young woman with a blond pageboy and frosted lipstick who looked a little dazed, as if she'd just woken up. She wheeled in a cart holding a machine with a tall plexiglass cylinder and a thick suction hose. She sat by my feet and told me to open my legs. She told me the machine would make a lot of noise. She told me it would hurt, but that they would give me some drugs so that I would not remember anything later on. This struck me as a bad sort of compromise. But in fact, all I did remember, afterward, was my bluish-purple blood spattering against the cylinder's walls.

We spent most of the night in the ER. Every time I tried to sit up, black static fingers stretched before my eyes and I had to lie down again. When I began to shake, they covered me with blankets. The lights were uniformly bright, but I knew time had passed because the first nurse disappeared and another one took over. The new nurse wore green scrubs and clogs and had a German accent. She thought I might be having an adverse reaction to the pain meds they'd given me, but instead we discovered, after a long while, that I was simply dehydrated. I went through two IV bags of fluids, drank a couple of glasses of water, stood weakly, and went home.

The sky was just flattening to pale gray over the mountains when we got back to the house. I didn't get out of bed until late the next afternoon.

6.

*If you really find out what you are, you will see that you are
not an individual, you are not a person, you are not a body.*
— Nisargadatta Maharaj

Eventually, the body reverts. Or maybe you forget,
or both. Time doubled and redoubled—I passed through
what would have been trimesters, week by week, and slowly,
I began to feel like what I thought of as "myself" again. At
least, I fit into my old clothes. My stomach flattened. I cut
my hair.

Every so often, though, someone who hadn't heard
the news would ask me when the baby was due, and I would
have to say, even though it should have been obvious by
just looking at me, "There is no baby," and they would look
confused and then embarrassed and then they'd say, "Oh, I'm
sorry," but I could see they didn't really understand.

My husband and I agreed to try again, but for a long
time we didn't have sex. When we finally did, I began to cry.
He touched my hair and said, "I had no idea you were still
feeling so upset by all this."

I took a class in which there was a pregnant woman.
Over the course of the semester, I watched her grow round
and heavy, her shirts stretched too tight across her chest, a
roll of flesh showing about her waist. Her cheeks plumped,
her upper arms grew fat. She brought food to class—bags
of cookies and nuts and dried fruit, steaming mugs of decaf
tea—which she arranged before her on the table we all sat
around. She wasn't feeling sick at all, she said. She talked
about herself incessantly, the way I knew I had too, as if no
one had ever experienced a pregnancy quite this way before.
I overheard her in the hall, after class, going on about her
midwife and pre-natal yoga and Bradley versus Lamaze. I
didn't want to hate her but I did. I put my head down and
looked away.

95

7.

An ancient patriarch said, "After enlightenment you are still the same as you were before. There is no mind and there is no truth." When you have arrived at this recognition, please hold on to it.

—Pai-Chang

Right around what should have been my due date, I got pregnant again. This time I told nobody. I ran the water while I threw up, pretended to sip my wine. I marked nothing in my date book, made no plans. Through my skylight, the winter sun refracted through frost etched on the glass. I sat on the floor where the blinds cast white stripes onto the carpet and worked on the breathing exercises I'd learned. I inhaled through my right (solar) nostril and out through the (lunar) left. I inhaled through both nostrils, then held the breath at the back of my throat for as long as I could bear. I breathed in through my curled tongue and exhaled through my nose. I drew the air into my lungs and held it there, listening to the humming inside my head. It was the sound that lay beneath all other sounds, a distant thumping, like a drum or a giant heart. It said: Hold on. It said: Let go.

AFTERIMAGE

We are packing up the house. The air is pulpy with the smells of cardboard and newsprint, and every room is lined with boxes, flaps fanned open at the top. We pack and pack— eighty boxes already, and so far, with two weeks still to go, we haven't missed a thing. What do we keep it all for? Books and more books, unused wedding presents and mismatched wine glasses, worn-out stuffed animals and outgrown toys, sheaves of letters, boxes of loose photographs, a landfill of sweaters, shoes and clothes: the weighty apparatus of four lives. It will take more than 200 book boxes, dish barrels, mirror boxes, mattress crates, a football field of paper, Bubble Wrap and tape to contain it all. We want to contain it. We want to hold it tight.

This morning, it is raining, a passing early storm. Water rustles through the cottonwood leaves, drips in beaded rivulets off the overhang above the porch. A low roll of thunder murmurs in the distance, raindrops pling against the hood vent of the stove. A thick band of cloud has descended over the Wasatch so that it looks as if there are no mountains there at all, as if the house might have lifted off from Salt Lake City and spun itself around while we were sleeping and set us down in the flatlands of the Midwest, which soon will be our home.

There's no place like home, Dorothy chants, clicking her ruby heels as she recites her dream-dissolving spell. I've moved half a dozen times since I first left my parents' house for college, twenty-five years ago this fall, and sometimes I wonder if there is any place I'll ever really feel at home. I feel loose-footed on this spinning planet, as displaced as those mountains vanished in the fog. Of course, you don't have to move physically to leave yourself behind. Something is lost with every tick of the second hand on the clock.

97

I sit here now at the kitchen table with my notebook, a mug of coffee warm between my hands, my husband tapping at the computer in the next room, the children still asleep upstairs, and I want to say that I'll never forget it, this moment—the cloud draped low over the mountains, the drip-drip of spring rain—but even as I write these words, it is gone.

*

Twice a week in yoga class, I sit cross-legged on the floor, eyes closed, trying to turn my gaze inward to the brow point, the sixth chakra *anja*, the third eye. Opening the third eye, I've read, brings insight, self-knowledge, intuitive understanding, the ability to "see" beyond the physical world. I like the idea of clairvoyance, of course, but I find I have a hard time holding my attention on the pulsating universe behind my lids. What is that grainy galaxy, backlit by a reddish glow, sparked with points of white? Is it the inner lining of the eyelid or the residue of refracted light? I'm distracted by the musky smell of incense, by the rustling of my classmates on their mats, by thoughts of the cone and rod cells of the eye, of the pea-shaped pineal gland nestled deep between the hemispheres of the brain. Some say the gland— which regulates the body's circadian rhythms in response to perceived patterns of darkness and light, and whose cells indeed bear a strong resemblance to optic photoreceptors—is related to the third eye. I try again to focus my closed eyes, turned upward and slightly crossed, on a point somewhere between my brows. I inhale in three short sniffs, then breathe out slowly, noisily, pushing the air against the back of my throat. A black orb wavers briefly in the center of my field of vision, disappears.

"When your mind wanders, bring it back," the instructor intones. Back where? I try to stay in the moment— with the breath swelling in my lungs, my heart tap-tapping behind my ribs—but rising before me instead is the sun-rimmed window of my childhood bedroom, dust motes dancing in the hazy light, my mother's footfall creaking on the stairs. The images are less memory than sensation. They move, unbidden, ectoplasmic, like floaters, those darting strands of protein you only notice when you fix your gaze on something white. When you try to look at them directly, they slip away.

Fragments of memory, known as engrams, are thought to take the form of physical or biochemical changes to the neuronal networks of the brain. It is believed that engrams are triggered by external stimuli, but researchers do not understand precisely how or where the memory traces are stored. Some neuropsychologists hypothesize that engrams are produced by the hallucinogenic chemical dimethyltryptamine, secreted by the pineal gland. The fact is, it's easier to feel that I am there in that long-vanished childhood morning than it is to conjure, with my eyes closed, a clear image of the yoga studio in which I sit. So which place is more real?

*

My parents still live in the house where I grew up, and my childhood room remains much the way I left it when I last lived there at eighteen. It's a shrine to my long-vanished child-self, a garden gone to seed, a tangle of dusty paperbacks, knickknacks and disheveled dolls. My mother refuses to throw any of it away, although from time to time she urges me to come and weed things out myself.

"I don't want to leave you with a mess to clean up when I die," she says. Now that we're moving, she says, it's time.

Back in Boston, I shake open a large black trash bag and sit down on the floor of my old room. From a built-in cabinet, I exhume a postcard of Baryshnikov mid-leap, a silver-plated pendant in the shape of a Hershey's Kiss, faded mimeographs of high school class songs and summer reading lists, stacks of letters, a flowered fabric-covered scrapbook (blank). I remember each of these objects perfectly, though I haven't thought about them in years. I take a breath, open the trash bag, and stuff them in.

My mother comes in and perches on the edge of the bed. "You don't need to throw *everything* away, you know," she says, reaching for a postcard with a cartoon of a girl with googly eyes on the front and my paternal grandmother's spidery handwriting on the back. *My most beloved darling.* August 1970. I would have been seven then, the same age as my daughter now. Will we be sitting together like this, looking at postcards from my own mother, when my daughter is forty-three?

My mother says, "You know, you only need to get rid of those things you don't want to keep."

What don't I want? I fish the pendant out of the trash bag, fingering the Kiss's paper pull-tab, which reads *I Love You,* and which, amazingly, is still intact. I give it to my daughter, along with the scrapbook and a doll with floozy blond hair and tattered clothes, and pack them all into yet another box to be shipped to our new Ohio home. I retrieve the letters, the postcards, the mimeographs. I open the cabinet and put them back.

To my surprise, my mother is satisfied with this. In fact, she seems relieved. "Everything will be here for you whenever you want it," she says.

*

Our bodies carry little with them through the years. The cells of the epidermis, the surface layer of the skin, shed and renew themselves entirely every two weeks or so. The epithelial cells that line the gut last only about five days; red blood cells, four months; liver cells, a year. At the cellular level, a typical adult's body may be, on average, a mere seven to ten years old. Every decade we are new! The long-lived have nine lives after all, like cats. The only parts of the body that endure from birth to death, scientists believe, are the neurons of the cerebral cortex, the inner lens cells of the eye, and the muscles of the heart. Even the neural structures of the hippocampus, where memories of names and places are first inscribed, regenerate themselves, do not persist. We are, quite literally, not the same people from day to day, from one year to the next. We're constantly casting ourselves off, starting over fresh.

Maybe that's the reason we hang on to all those boxes of old letters and half-filled notebooks and long-forgotten toys, lugging them from cabinet to cabinet, attic to attic, never unpacking them, never throwing them away. They're the lost substance of our bodies, the stuff of vanished time.

*

Even though my daughter has learned to read a clock, we tussle over bedtime nearly every night. There is a part of me that hates for her to lose the child's wondrous ability to experience the contraction and dilation of the moment, the infinite plasticity of time. Still, it's nearly nine o'clock, and she's a kid who needs her sleep.

I pry her away from the 500-piece jigsaw puzzle she's just decided to launch into and herd her up the stairs to bed. Even before we reach the top, she is in full-on meltdown mode. Everything I say just makes it worse. I hear my mother's voice coming out of my own mouth—*You're just overtired; tomorrow's another day; settle down now and go to sleep!*—as I wrestle her into her pajamas. I remember the hot flush of my own childhood belligerence over going to bed.

"I *hate* you!" my daughter screams, red in the face, tears streaming down her overtired cheeks. "You're the *worst*! I'm going to pack my suitcase and run away!"

Out in the hallway, my husband shrugs. "All kids say stuff like that," he says. "My sister had this little suitcase with orange flowers on it that she'd pack up when she got really mad. She'd haul it down to the empty lot at the end of the street and sit on it, her chin propped on her fists."

I lean against the wall, listening to my daughter's sobs, almost in tears myself. How did I become *the worst*?

"It was pretty funny," my husband says.

I picture my daughter's empty drawers, the hangers jangling in her closet, the hollow indentation in her bed. "So what did your parents do?" I say.

"Oh, nothing," he says. "After a little while, she'd get bored and sneak back home again."

*

As it happens, I, too, had a little orange-flowered suitcase with a white plastic handle and four white-button legs, but I don't remember ever packing it to run away. I was terrified of spending even a night away from home and refused for years to go on sleepovers or away to camp. The fear began the year I turned eight, the year of my long-anticipated brother's birth. He was a four-pound preemie who survived an intrauterine blood transfusion for severe Rh disease and had to spend two weeks in an incubator at the Boston Lying-In. Children under thirteen weren't allowed to visit the hospital in those days, but with the nurses' encouragement, my father sneaked me in through the emergency room, down a subterranean hallway lined with chirring washing machines and steamy banks of dryers, and up a cavernous service elevator to the special care nursery, where I knelt on a chair and peered through a plate-glass window at the rows of newborns in their little plastic boxes, like animals in the zoo. My brother was jaundiced and nearly bald, with wrinkled, too-loose skin, like the Great Dane puppy our neighbors had brought home a few years before. He was naked except for a diaper and a hospital band cinched around his ankle like the tag on the leg of an endangered bird. On the opposite side of the glass, my mother reached into the incubator and cradled him in the palm of her hand. The nurses and the other visitors cooed and fussed.

My fear of sleepovers began on the day my parents brought my brother home. I had gone to spend the night at a friend's house; my mother thought it would be easier to get the baby settled in if I wasn't there. What I remember is lying in my sleeping bag on the floor in my friend's playroom, unable to sleep. The vaulted room above the garage was cluttered with toys that cast misshapen shadows in the dark. Panic swelled like helium in my chest, made me gasp for air, although I couldn't have said what the matter was even if I could have spoken through my choking tears. My friend stood by, helplessly twisting her hair. Finally, at her suggestion, I got up and called my mother from the telephone on the playroom wall and begged her to come and take me home, wailing into the receiver as, in a distant, faded voice, she told me go to sleep, that she would see me in the morning, that everything would be all right. Later, she talked to me about green-eyed jealousy, unconscious fears of being abandoned or displaced. Even so, it would be years before I slept over at a friend's house again.

The morning after my daughter's meltdown, she has forgotten all about her threat to run away. She comes downstairs and wraps her arms around my hips and presses her sleepy face against my belly and tells me that when she grows up she wants to live with her little brother in the house next door so that they can visit us every day. I glance out the window at the bungalow next to ours. The woman who lives there has Alzheimer's; from time to time we have found her wandering along the street, disoriented and confused, and have gone out and gently steered her home. She smiles at us vacantly these days, not remembering who we are. Soon someone else will be standing at this window, looking out at her, at the house my children would like to imagine someday will be theirs. I root around in a cardboard box to find one of the notebooks I have already packed away, and then I write my daughter's comment down so that I won't forget.

*

By now the morning rain has eased up a bit, though the fog still hasn't lifted off the valley floor. I squint past the power lines and over the neighboring roofs and trees to the place where the rocky flanks of Millcreek Canyon and Olympus Cove should be, but still there's nothing there but clouds, a flat and gray extension of the sky. It doesn't even seem possible that the mountains still exist. Already I miss them: the glint of snow on the upper reaches of Mount Olympus, the foothills warming from gray to brownish-green. I love the way they hover, pale as wisps of cloud, on ice-blue winter mornings; the way the highest peaks, framed in my upstairs skylight, turn pinkish-orange in the alpenglow. I want to touch the mountains with my glance the way you reach into your pocket to touch a lucky stone. It's the *image* of the mountains that I love, more than anything: the simple fact of their existence, their solid presence against the cloud-swept sky.

I download a new screen saver for my computer, a photograph of an unidentified Utah peak, luminous in the blue light of a full moon. Once we've left this place, what difference will it make to look at it instead?

*

Perception, scientists say, creates a figure that is not a property of the object being observed but the result of the organization of sensations by the "mind's eye," the brain. We "see" when refracted light focuses, upside down, on the retina, stimulating a chemical reaction in the 125,000,000 rod and cone cells of the fovea, and generating an electrical impulse that travels first through the ganglion neurons and then the optic nerve to the visual cortex of the brain, which then turns the inverted image right side up, merging the differential data from each eye. What we see is not unmediated "reality" at all.

I scroll through images of the eye's physiology on my computer, color photographs and scientific sketches that might as well be dispatches from Mars. Observed through a slit lamp biomicroscope, the retina glows like a harvest moon, the optic disc—the blind spot where the optic fibers leave the eye—a brilliant yellow-orange orb striated with crimson arteries and veins. Magnified, the nerve cells of the retina look uncannily like plant life: floating tendrils of ferny nerve fibers, cattail-like axons, dendrites like bubble-studded bladder wrack or spreading cedar boughs. It's a strange thrill to peer into the wild landscape of the eye.

Lately my mother's vision has become flecked with floaters, opaque squiggles that dart like filaments of hair or dust across the vitreous collagen that fills the back of the eye. Sometimes, she says, a gray veil moves across her field of vision, like a ghost. Her retinas are tearing at the edges, pulling away from the back of the eyeball like wallpaper peeling off a wall. She sees things slightly blurred around the edges, sees occasional flashes of bright light. She may need surgery to prevent her from going blind. I wonder if I, too, will experience disturbances to my vision as I age. Even now I wonder how much of what I think I see is really there at all.

*

Packing, I come across an old Brownie-box snapshot of my husband as a baby, seated outdoors in a high chair beneath the broad boughs of a pine. He's so tiny in the picture you can barely make out his face, but there's a good view of the house and yard. My husband's parents, like my own, still live in the house in which he grew up (although unlike me, he's kept nothing there). We show the picture to the kids, pointing out the way things used to be: the neighbor's gardens stretching down the hill, the addition not yet added on, the porch not yet closed in. We exchange a glance over the children's heads. We're thinking how they won't be able to look at pictures of their childhood home like this. They won't even remember living here.

My father and his family left Nazi-occupied Europe when he was a boy of nine. My mother's father brought nine members of his family out of Lithuania to the United States around the same time. They packed what they could pack and left the rest behind. They were exiles from their homelands, refugees. We are none of those things. We're moving because we want to, for a new job. But I've moved enough to know that even if you're not in exile, Thomas Wolfe was right: You can't go home again.

"How will we fit all our stuff onto the airplane?" my four-year-old son wants to know. "Will we take the refrigerator? The walls? The cars? The doors? The beds?" Even to my own ears, my explanations sound a little lame. Why is it that we'll take the cars but not the fridge? The Christmas cactus but not the strawberry plant in the backyard, the tricycle but not the sandbox, the wagon but not the swing? What will happen to the things we leave behind? Will they retain any trace that we were here?

My son and I walk around together with the digital camera and fill up the entire memory card. Then he sits on my lap in front of the computer and we watch the slideshow play. The pictures flash onto the screen, and already it feels as if we're looking at images from the distant past, even though in reality only a few minutes have gone by since I snapped the shots. The yard seems unnaturally bright, the kitchen underexposed and dim. Those U-Haul boxes show up in every frame. My son wriggles around to face me, the corners of his mouth pulled down.

"Mommy," he says. "It doesn't look the same."

*

Freud once famously described a game his eighteen-month-old grandson liked to play with a wooden spool tied to a piece of string. *O-o-o-o!* the boy would cry, throwing the spool over the side of his crib so that it disappeared. *Fort!* Gone! Then, cooing with pleasure, he'd reel it in. *Da!* Here! To Freud the game represented the child's way of coping with the separation anxiety caused by his mother's absences. The disappearing, reappearing spool of string reassured the boy that the vanished object would return, providing a fantasy of control. Language, of course, also conjures things that are not here, re-presents them, brings them back. *Gone, here.* Even words are an act of faith.

It is the footnote on the next page that blows me away. Almost as an afterthought, Freud writes that the empowerment associated with the Fort/Da game may help account for his grandson's lack of emotional reaction to his mother's death, just a few years later on.

His mother's death.

I have to stop and read that passage a couple of times.

107

*

A large red Conté crayon drawing by Hyman Bloom titled *The Séance* hangs in my parents' front hall. The medium is a young woman, her lips curved in a knowing, secret smile. She gazes out of the upper-left quadrant of the canvas, her open eyes focused far off, beyond the frame. Around her, disembodied faces float in varying degrees of definition—some no more than rough crosshatched strokes, others shaded in finely drawn detail. The face rendered most fully—a woman's face with high cheekbones and bowed lips, her deep-set eyes closed as if in sleep—is an uncanny double of my mom's.

My mother's mother died of cancer at thirty-seven when my mother was just thirteen, her brothers nine and four. As near as I can tell from photographs, the face in the drawing strongly resembles my grandmother's as well. I wonder if my mother thinks of her when she walks past that drawing every day, or whether, with time, she has managed to forget. My mother, at seventy, is in robust health; I can't begin to think about what it will be like when she is gone. And yet even now, when I close my eyes and turn them inward to my brow point, I can't produce the image of her face. All I come up with is a distorted afterimage, bright but featureless, like the luminous impression of a flash.

*

The existence of forgetting has never been proved, Nietzsche once wrote. *We only know that some things don't come to mind when we want them.* I want to believe that we don't forget, that memory is inscribed on those long-lasting cerebral cortex cells of ours like a palimpsest, traces of a painting covered by a more recent artist's paint. I want to believe that the hidden pigments remain there, shadowy as ghosts, waiting for the conservator's X-ray to bring them back.

Memory is kinetic, after all: the substance of our muscles, not just our minds. I imagine all the things I've ever forgotten bubbling beneath a transparent barrier stretched across my brain, like molecules bumping against the myelin membrane of a cell. It's comforting to think they're there, even if they can't be accessed, a question of organization, not of loss.

In one of those boxes of mementos I've been carting around for years, I come across a handwritten note in French. *Quand te reverrai-je?* it reads, continuing—in rhyming couplets, no less!—*Avant de nous quitter fais moi un petit mot / Pour me dire que tu partages / Mon sentiment et votre image.* It's dated (September 8, 1986) and signed, although I can't make out the name, which might be Emil, or perhaps Eric. It's possible that I was in Paris with my boyfriend then, but nothing about this apparent love note rings a bell. Not even a faint tinkle. Who could this Gallic paramour have been? Was he cute? Were we drunk? Did we kiss? It feels as if it must be close, this missing memory, but it will not come back, the way a face cut out of a photograph leaves a head-shaped hole.

*

The sky is bright now over the Wasatch to the east; over the Oquirrhs, to the west, it's a cloud-swept baby blue. The mountains have reappeared as well, of course, solid and gray-brown at the lower elevations, with a dusting of fresh snow across the higher peaks. This morning's storm reminds me how long it's been since we've had a real daylong downpour, the kind that makes you want to curl up on the couch with a good book. Here in the high desert you can watch the storms swelling like dark herds far off over the lake; they stampede across the valley and then are gone, the puddles drying up before the kids get home to splash. Maybe in Ohio we'll have those long, wet days of my East Coast childhood again—the smells of mud and sodden leaves and pondweed and rusty screens, the steady patter of raindrops against the glass.

Are we different people depending on where we are? I'm thinking of Chopin, humming Polish mazurkas at the piano in Paris; or Chekhov, writing about the windblown Russian steppe from beneath the palms in Nice. Do we have to travel, like Dorothy, all the way to Oz to see clearly the place we've come from? It seems to me that the world is made up of plural, parallel realities that shift and slide over one another like the lenses in an optometrist's phoropter. We're always in more than one place at a time.

What do you see now, out that window, beyond the glass, beyond the frame? Those mountains? They're nothing but a trick of Renaissance perspective, an illusion of three-dimensionality projected onto a flat plane. They're an electrical signal transmitted on a neuron, projected upside down on your retina, righted by your brain. Close your eyes and turn them inward toward your brow point, *anja*, the third eye. Picture a different landscape: a rolling hillside thick with scrub oaks and maples, buzzards reeling overhead, a canopy of autumn leaves—russet, yellow, orange-red—silhouetted against a cotton sky. Toss the spool and reel it back. *Fort, da.* Blink, and it is gone.

A NATURAL HISTORY OF SMALL-TOWN OHIO

Like the rest of us, you come from elsewhere: on a wagon train across the Appalachians, on foot like Johnny Appleseed, on an airplane, in a beat-up car. You arrive with stacks of book-filled boxes, a sheaf of expectations, a moving van and children, or nothing but a rumpled map. You're spinning like a maple seed, wind-buoyed, adrift.

On Google Earth, this place is just a swath of green, a finger's length from the yellow ribbon of the interstate, two fingers from the nearest city sprawl. Zoom in and watch it morph into a quilt of pixelated squares. You know it from Saul Steinberg's famous *New Yorker* cover cartoon: that flat, foreshortened no-man's-land crosshatched in ochre pencil, stretching from the far border of the Hudson to the blue Pacific shore.

Click your heels three times and you'll be there.

*

The first thing you see as you approach is the bell tower of the college chapel, rising like a preacher's pointed finger above a ridge of evergreens. All around are rolling fields—lush ripples in the spring and summer, shorn to stubble in the winter, studded with collapsing barns and wheels of hay. Cross the train tracks and head down the hill, past the lumberyard, the corn mill, the early-settlers' burial ground with its tilting graves, to the intersection of Main and Broadway, the village's cross-shaped heart. There's a church on every corner: rusticated neo-Gothic spires for the founding Baptists, blocks of tawny sandstone for the Presbyterians, pinkish stucco for the Methodists, white Ionic columns along the Episcopalians' classical facade. The Lutherans, Catholics, Mormons, Evangelical Baptists, and Seventh Day Adventists are here as well, at the edges of the town.

You didn't exactly think you'd find a synagogue, but still, you hadn't quite expected this. Feel the collision of tectonic plates, the shift of schist and shale.

*

Here at the edge of the Allegheny plateau, the earth has heaved and folded, drained and split. Once mastodons grazed these hillsides, and prehistoric tribes mounded the earth into giant geometric configurations aligned with the moon and stars. The Welsh and English settlers who trekked west from Massachusetts at the turn of the nineteenth century found in this wooded landscape a place that reminded them of home. You feel strangely at home, as well. It's all uncannily familiar: the trim Victorians and historic inns, the dappled summer mornings, the brick-and-ivy campus, the maples flaming in the fall.

But these Appalachian foothills are not the Berkshires; these flooded creeks and cow ponds are no New England lakes. To the west, soybean and corn fields stretch to Indiana, Iowa, Nebraska—the flat and foreign heart of the Midwest. It makes you think of the time when, as a child, trailing your mother through the produce aisle of the grocery store, you reached for the hem of her blue coat and trotted along beside her until she stopped, and you looked up and found a stranger's face instead.

"And who are you?" the stranger said.

Your mother was just over *there*, examining the tomatoes; she was not really lost at all. But in that moment, the familiar cracked. A trapdoor opened underneath you, and you fell.

*

In the backyard, the children discover fossils embedded on the surface of broken sandstone slabs: the tiny doughnut imprint of a crinoid, a screw-like bryozoan, a brachiopod's perfect fan-shaped shell. In the Devonian era, this wooded hillside—500 miles from the Atlantic, a hundred miles from even the southernmost Great Lake—lay at the bottom of an inland sea. The departing waters left their mark in this soil limned with fossils, in this fertile loam.

In college, you knew a boy from Montana who kept asking what it was like to grow up in Boston, as if you must have been a different kind of person, coming from a place that opened onto water, perched on the ocean's edge. Now the coasts are out of sight. *Landlocked*, your relatives used to say, with a shudder, when talking about the Midwest.

In the womb, remember, we are all water creatures first. Oh, to unzip the skin, to shed the layers of accretion, to stream through water like an eel!

*

Everything grows here. The woods are leafy, dense with underbrush and thorny saplings fighting toward the light. In spring the air swirls green with pollen. You learn the names of trees you never knew before: buckeye, alder, locust, redbud, larch. You learn to distinguish the lacy flowers of Queen Anne's lace from cowbane, to pick out poison ivy's three-fingered spread. The deer meander through the yard, nipping off the lily buds, nibbling the hosta, like heads of lettuce, right down to the stems. They won't touch the spiny Canada thistle, the purple-flowered joe-pye weed, the thick clusters of crown vetch.

113

There's no botanical definition of a weed. They're just outsiders, ugly and unwanted, crowding out the native species with their invasive sprawl. They thrive on change, adapt. In the carbon dioxide–rich air of our warming planet, it's said they'll grow to twice their normal height. Split the taproot of a weed, and new shoots will sprout from the shattered fragments left behind.

*

Around the neighbors' pool, as the children whoop and splash, the women chatter about Bible camp; the men, holding cans of Natural Light, talk football, ATVs. You feel pale and awkward in your newness, surrounded by these jolly people in their baseball caps and brightly-colored shirts. They're all friends from church.

"And where are you from?" they ask, with their flat Midwestern vowels, their faces open and bright. They say, "It must be different for you here."

Later that evening, after you've gone home to put the kids to bed, your four-year-old calls to you, frightened— there's an alien in his room.

"Go to sleep!" you call back.

But when you go to him, annoyed, you find that you are wrong: Two weird eyes hover, disembodied, in the shadows above his bed. They are fluorescent green, these eyes, and tiny—little blinking flares. For a moment, you freeze. Then you realize: fireflies.

Catch them between your palms and take them outside, set them free. They drift upward into the summer darkness, flashing like sparks stirred from a dying fire, and vanish on the wind.

*

In this year that marks the bicentennial of the village's founding, the Fourth of July parade stretches for two miles along Broadway. People crowd along the sidewalks, waving flags. The children grab for candy tossed from passing floats. Judges and politicians wave from banner-festooned cars; high school reunion classmates cheer from wagons piled high with bales of hay. The 4-H band booms past: pimply boys puffing into trumpets, thick-legged cheerleaders twirling batons. The Pork Queen, in a dime-store tiara and strapless satin gown, perched on a rusty pickup, genteelly turns her palm. A troupe of men in moth-eaten Civil War uniforms halt and load their muskets, fire sulfurous blanks into the air. People ride by on tractors, big-wheeled tricycles, lawn mowers, ponies, vintage automobiles. Hook and ladder trucks and pumpers, ambulances, and squad cars whoop their sirens, gleaming in the sun. Women in sunbonnets and gingham dresses trail behind a spinet piano mounted on a wagon, singing hymns in harmony as they pass out flyers proclaiming *Jesus Saves*.

There were no Jews here in 1805, of course, when the founding fathers first mapped out the tidy routes of Broadway and Maple Street and Elm. Back then, your great-great-grandparents were still in Moravia and Lithuania and Belarus, peddling *schmattes* or bending over Talmud scrolls in the *shul*. In photographs, they stand grim-faced in black coats and high-necked dresses, gazing blindly at you from the past. America, to them, would have been nothing but a story—*Ohio* just a primitive vowel sound around which to wrap their lips.

Even now, hardly anyone is Jewish here. Wave your flag and smile. Hold your children's hands. Feel the ground beneath your feet.

*

In 1860, a local man digging in the Indian mounds uncovered two pieces of stone inscribed with Hebrew text. One was a small limestone block, shaped like a mezuzah or phylactery, bearing the image of a bearded Moses and a version of the Ten Commandments, the Decalogue, carved into the stone. The other, keystone-shaped, was inscribed with Hebrew phrases: *Qedosh Qedoshim, Melekh Eretz, Torath YHWH, Devor YHWH.*

To some, the stones seemed proof that the Hopewell Indian mounds—the largest and most sophisticated prehistoric earthworks in the world—could not have been built by heathen savages. Local clergy thrilled to the idea that the Mound Builders might have actually been Hebrews descended from the Lost Tribes of Israel, to the promise of a link between this new and wild continent and the Bible's ancient land. It's a notion that still appeals to some today, even though there can be little doubt that the so-called "Newark Holy Stones" are fakes. The peculiar script of the inscriptions, scholars say, is a form of post-exilic Hebrew that could not have been produced by a pre-Columbian Lost Tribe. The lettering contains the kinds of errors an unschooled copyist plausibly might make. The robed and bearded Moses is not characteristic of the ancient Hebrews' images at all.

Consider the stones in their display case at the Johnson-Humrickhouse Museum in Coshocton, perched on their little Lucite stands atop a crimson carpet square. The Decalogue stone looks less like a mezuzah than a tiny tombstone, its limestone case a coffin with a lid. But the Hebrew letters spell out words you know. Words that don't belong here.

Nail a mezuzah to the right-hand doorpost of your house, as the Torah prescribes. The slender silver case contains twenty-two Hebrew lines from Deuteronomy inscribed on a square of parchment furled into a scroll—a prayer you never learned to read. Press your fingers to your lips and touch it anyway, to bless your home, the way your great-great-grandparents would have once touched theirs.

*

Here in the Ohio River valley, the weather is stronger, closer, wilder than anything you've known before: a consuming, almost biblical force. There are ice storms, wind storms, tornadoes, blizzards, floods. High winds rip the copper steeple off the Lutheran church, send street signs hurtling like boomerangs, split and topple trees. The power fails and stays out for seven days. At night, you read by candlelight, the darkness draped around you like a shroud.

Tornado sirens split the quiet of a September afternoon. The children hide in a downstairs bathroom, clutching their stuffed animals, while your husband sits on the couch upstairs, drinking a beer, watching the eastward progress of the thunderstorms outlined in vivid red-and-yellow Doppler radar on TV. Outside, the wind is rising, a premonitory roar. Leaves flash silver in the electric air. The rain approaches like a beaded screen. Soon torrents are overflowing the gutters, cascading down the windows, turning the world into a blur. Lighting strikes so close, the whole house shakes.

Later, you find the evidence: a ten-foot splinter sheared off a neighbor's pine. A singed scar runs the length of the trunk. The exposed wood looks pale and vulnerable, like the raw flesh of a wound.

In the slanting sunlight, a swirl of milkweed spores rises in the shape of the Big Dipper, as if even the stars have been knocked loose by the storm.

*

Roadkill is everywhere: squirrels, chipmunks, woodchucks, blackbirds, skunks, and deer. Buzzards wheel above the trees. You skirt the bloody pulp of fur and bone as you walk past, raising a cloud of flies. The doe's glassy eye is fixed; the woodchuck's black-nailed paws are stiff. One autumn night, driving home along a country road, your husband hits a buck, sends it cartwheeling across the windshield into the woods along the verge. The car is totaled. But when you return to the site of the accident the next morning, the deer is gone.

On clear days, robins hurl themselves against your plate glass windows, mistaking the reflection of the sky for air. You find a dead one in a clump of ferns. You scoop it onto a piece of cardboard and carry it to the woods along the hill. It feels surprisingly light, blush-bellied, its wings splayed.

"Shouldn't you have buried it?" the children want to know. "Shouldn't you say a prayer?" The words of the Mourner's Kaddish come to mind: *Yit'gadal veyit'kadash sh'mei raba.* It's not really a prayer for the dead at all, of course, but a reminder of the awesome might of God.

*

At first you barely notice them: small brown spirals, coiled like watch springs, dried up beneath the bed or on the bathroom floor. You don't connect them to the slender, dark-brown, worm-like creatures with a fuzz of legs that you sometimes find alive and crawling, their heads swiveling like the tip of fiber-optic catheters. It's not until your husband crushes one beneath his shoe that you realize where that smell's been coming from that's been plaguing you for weeks. It's foul and sweet, the smell of something rotting, almost like feces, but not quite. You've already thrown out the bathroom wastebasket, had the plumber change the toilet seal. You must have vacuumed them up unwittingly; now the vacuum, too, emits the awful smell.

You look them up and learn that they are millipedes: thousand-legged creatures who feed on moist, decomposing vegetation, of which there's no shortage in your shady yard. When threatened, you discover, certain species emit a form of hydrocyanide gas to repel enemies.

Cyanide gas. You can't help but think, *like Zyklon B.*

It's not like other unpleasant smells you stop noticing after a little bit. It lingers in the air for days.

*

Out for drinks with a group of women friends, the conversation turns to the prayer meetings held beneath the high school flagpole, the "abstinence-only" Sex Ed curriculum, the unfriendly looks one woman's dark-skinned husband gets at a local bar. The woman sitting next to you—a pretty redhead with a freckled nose—leans over with a smile and says that, growing up, she always wished that she were Jewish, too. You understand that, by *Jewish,* she means *exotic, different,* like a geisha, maybe, or Scheherazade. You feel conscious, suddenly of your greenish eyes, your brownish hair, your smallish nose. "But you don't look Jewish," people used to tell you, growing up. You took that the way they meant it—as a compliment. So what exactly does this woman see?

Just half an hour away, on the east side of the city, there are synagogues and ethnic restaurants and people with the skin and languages of every race. Maybe it would be better, you think, to raise your children there, in a place that's more diverse, a place where they'll fit in.

You understand that, by *fitting in,* you mean: with people who are just like you.

119

*

Your neighbor traps raccoons in his backyard. He leaves the animal in the trap all day, "to set an example," he says, "for the rest." You're not sure whether or not he means this as a joke. Later, his twelve-year-old son drowns the raccoon in a garbage can.

Out the window of the school bus, the children spot a hunter in camouflage gear, carrying a compound bow, stepping out of the woods just up the street. The village has permitted bow hunting in an effort to thin the overpopulation of deer. The chairwoman of the village council assures you that the hunters are well trained. You make your children play indoors.

The deer have been pushed into the village because the farmers are selling off their fields. Developers are filling the former corn and soybean fields with tract houses. Ersatz captain's walks look onto dry land as far as you can see. Man-made ponds spout geysers; white picket fences border acres of green turf. Road crews dig a new four-lane highway to the city. The old farmhouses and barns along its path are boarded up, destroyed. The land is leveled, rolled, and paved.

Thirteen percent of the people in this county live below the poverty line. One town away, the unemployment rate tops ten percent, and three out of ten kids do not finish high school. In nearby Buckeye Lake, catfish wash up dead along the muddy shore. A Superfund site abuts the village wells, the ground contaminated with a plume of chlorinated ethenes leaching from solvents stored in decaying buried drums. Radon gas seeps into basements through the underlying shale. Buzzards spiral overhead. It is said the frogs have nearly disappeared.

Down the road, a man plants in his yard a dozen rows of little orange flags, hundreds of them, one for every Ohio soldier killed in Afghanistan and Iraq. The flags flutter in the breeze as you drive by.

*

Despite the hunters, the deer—a huge buck with a damaged antler, half a dozen does and fawns—continue to tromp across your yard day after day, nibbling the hosta and the lilies. You clap your hands and shout, but they just gaze back at you with their curiously placid stare. A fat-bottomed woodchuck burrows beneath the deck, leaves his tooth marks along the rail. Raccoons maneuver beneath the bungee cord strapped over the garbage can and strew trash around the yard. Your son wakes to find a field mouse running in tight, demented circles around the floor next to his bed. Another morning, just outside the kitchen windows, there is a fox. A locust sapling pushes right through a crack in the concrete floor of the garage. At night, the darkness pulses with the descant creak of cicadas, the drone of katydids, a tomcat's yowl. Bats swoop like shadows through the trees. Moths beat against the windowpanes.

Give up your failed attempts to landscape and cheer them on instead—the deer and woodchucks, raccoons and mice, the weeds. Turn on the lights, throw open all the doors and windows, let the creatures in.

*

In your mind, you're elsewhere. Your dreams attach themselves to other landscapes, countries, cities, terrains. They twist like rivers, roiling into falls; they carry you to where the rivers meet the sea. In the rushing waters, you dissolve, float free.

But this isn't a dream. This is the place your children will name when people ask where they are from. This is the place to which, a hundred years from now, your great-great-grandchildren will trace their genealogy.

Wrap your lips around the vowels. Pucker up and say it: *O-hi-o*.

On a November night, you sit outside around a campfire, toasting marshmallows with the kids. Overhead, the old oaks stretch their branches across the cloud-dark sky. Think of the ancient Mound Builders huddled within their giant earthen octagon, their eyes turned to the stars. They are with you yet—in the particles of dirt beneath your feet, in the sparks that flicker upward through the darkness, in the molecules of air.

COUNTERCLOCKWISE

In my earliest memory, we are moving. I am three. I'm standing at the window of our Brookline, Massachusetts, apartment, looking down onto the street. There's the Dean Road playground with its dusty grass and metal slides and swings. There's my mother's car, pulled over to the curb, my mother getting in. The back seats are folded flat, packed with paintings which my father doesn't want to give to the movers. And then the car is pulling away, and I am wailing. Behind me, in the shadows beyond recollection, the living room walls stand strange and white and bare. They're not our walls without the paintings. Where has my mother taken them? When will she come back for me?

The new house is out in Natick, a dozen miles west. It's a turn-of-the-century white stucco on three acres by a pond, just off of the Mass Pike. The big front hall has a black-and-white chessboard floor, forest-green walls, a glinting chandelier. Beyond a central staircase, the wood-paneled, green-carpeted living room stretches into dimness. Upstairs, the bedroom that will be mine is painted yellow. My parents' room is lavender; an adjacent dressing room is gold. The kitchen is antacid pink. (The walls are *garish*, my mother says, under her breath. Soon they'll all be white.) In the basement, there's a billiards room with wagon-wheel light fixtures, dilapidated red leather banquettes, a fireplace with ceramic tiles depicting characters from *Alice in Wonderland*. In the new house, I feel like Alice, as if I've shrunken to be even smaller than I already am.

The sellers are an older couple named the Hirshbergs. The fact that they are Jewish seems to endear them to my parents, as if they're almost relatives, as if the house is not so much being purchased as bequeathed. They leave us furniture that won't fit into whatever smaller place they're moving to,

123

items that strike an eclectic contrast with my parents' Danish modern taste: heavy wooden bedroom sets, marble-topped side tables, throne-like wicker porch chairs, tall brass andirons topped with rams' heads, a mirrored vanity for my mother, a steel executive desk for my dad. For me, Mrs. Hirshberg brings out a doll-sized swing set, a 1950s "Ginny's Gym" that must have belonged to one of her by then grown-up kids. It has a wooden teeter-totter, a shiny slide, a baby swing. Mrs. Hirshberg shows me how to guide the Ginny doll down the slide and push her in the swing, but when I reach out to take the doll, Mrs. Hirshberg yanks her back. "No, no," she snaps. To my great disappointment, the doll's not mine to keep.

Without the doll, the swing set is useless. My baby doll is much too big, my other dolls too long and skinny, my stuffed animals likewise out of scale. The toy gathers dust at the back of my closet, where, for some reason, I feel a little guilty every time I notice that it's there.

It's the same feeling I get many years later when I come home to visit and see our real swing set on its grassy hillock next to the garage. The green wooden posts and rotting ladders. The lopsided, long-abandoned swings.

∞

My parents stay in that house long past the age the Hirshbergs were when they moved out. It seems as if everybody else's aging parents have downsized to single-story houses, independent or assisted living, condos in warmer climes. But my parents keep on dragging the trash bins out to the end of the long and rutted driveway, raking snow out of the gutters, climbing up and down the stairs. They go on squabbling about the trees in need of trimming and the lawn in need of mowing and the antiquated plumbing and the winter ice-dam leaks. My brother and I can't get them even to consider moving.

"Oh, no!" our mother says. "We manage very well!"

"But things could change," we point out. "What about Plan B?"

"There's no Plan B!" declares our father, waving a liver-spotted hand. "Plan B, we're dead!"

Like an enchanted briar thicket, our parents' house and all of their possessions have grown up around them, rooting them in place. There is the Eames chair in a corner of the living room, the Hirshbergs' marble-topped side tables, my grandmother's Gallé and Moser vases, the paintings and the sculptures, the closets full of silk ties and cashmere sweaters, the dusty wine bottles aging in the cellar, the acres of books, the Steinway baby grand. Our parents have worn deep grooves through routines that have not changed much over the past sixty years. My mother sips her afternoon tea at the kitchen table, reads in the comfortable chair in my brother's old room. My father sits at his desk, peers at the computer, calls friends and relatives on the phone. My mother takes her daily walk along the wooded path around the pond. My father makes his way down to the pool, where he takes a shady seat and thinks.

As much as I worry about my parents, the truth is I don't really want them to move. I like going home. For "home" the house remains to me, no matter how old I get or how long I live elsewhere.

The house, I come to see, is not, in fact, a house. It's a container of memory, a receptacle of time.

∞

In her famous 1979 "Counterclockwise" experiment, Harvard psychologist Ellen Langer sent eight men in their seventies to spend five days in a converted monastery in New Hampshire that had been set up to feel and look as if it were still 1959. Perry Como sang on the radio. *The Ed*

Sullivan Show played on a black-and-white TV. The books and magazines on the coffee table, the furniture and décor, were all carefully selected to match the style of twenty years before. The men were instructed not just to reminisce about the past, but to try to *be* the person they'd been then. They were told to talk about the news stories from 1959 as if they were current events. There were no mirrors, only photographs of their younger selves. Just one week later, Langer recorded marked improvements in all the testable biomarkers of age. The men's memory and grip strength improved, as did measures of vision, hearing, manual dexterity, gait, posture, flexibility, perception, cognition, memory, and IQ. Observers rated photos of the participants as appearing younger than before. On the last day, men who'd seemed almost too frail to walk just days earlier took up an impromptu game of football on the lawn.

In Langer's experiment, the mere *idea* of being twenty years younger seems to have a positive health effect. Power of mind over body? It's hard to say. (The study has not been replicated.) It seems to me, regardless, that my parents are in fact more energetic, sharper, and focused when they're at home, in the place they've lived for all these years. When they come to visit me, they move more tentatively, seem vaguer, more easily confused. And so I wonder: What if, like Langer's monastery, living in that house really does make my parents' psycho-biological clocks run a just little bit more slowly than they would elsewhere? What if the house is actually less of a looming health risk than the thing that's keeping them alive?

∞

We think of time as linear and constant, but it's not. As Einstein showed, time dilates, speeding up and slowing down with differentials in relative velocity and gravity. Time passes more slowly on fast-moving objects than on slower-moving objects. As experiments have proved, an ultraprecise atomic clock traveling on the International Space Station (at 17,500 mph and 200 miles altitude) will run about five milliseconds per year slower than a reference clock on Earth. Astronauts return from space just a tiny bit younger than the rest of us. Time also passes more quickly on weightless objects than on those subjected to a strong gravitational force. An atomic clock traveling on a GPS satellite (at just 7,000 mph but at 12,000 miles altitude) will run about fourteen milliseconds per year faster than an identical clock on Earth.

Our experience of time is also far from constant. It's distorted by our emotions, by the speed of our saccadic eye movements, by neurological changes in our aging brains. Time drags when we're bored, flies when we're having fun. Time is an opponent, or a commodity; we race time, kill time, steal time, borrow, buy, and spend time. We never quite feel in sync with our bodies as we age. My mother used to say that in her mind, she was always thirty-eight. Studies say that the vast majority of adults over forty feel, on average, twenty percent younger than they really are. As the years go by, I too mostly feel as if I haven't changed. Everybody else seems to be getting younger, instead.

I don't think I really believed that my father would die. Or maybe I just couldn't imagine what not having him would be like. Even at the very end, his pain finally tamped down by morphine, his features sunken, his last breaths rattling in his chest, I found I couldn't grasp that he was leaving. The hospice nurses gave me a knowing, pitying look. "It's time," they said. A cheap clock hung on the wall above his bed. It kept on ticking.

∞

In the famous opening scene of *Alice in Wonderland*, Alice is idling on a riverbank beside her sister when the White

Rabbit rushes past. Pulling a watch out of his waistcoat pocket, he cries, "Oh dear! Oh dear! I shall be late!" It's the rabbit's watch that catches Alice's attention, as "burning with curiosity, she ran across the field after it, and fortunately was just in time to see it pop down a large rabbit-hole under the hedge." The rush of time quite literally pulls Alice into Wonderland—a place where time doesn't function normally in the least.

In Wonderland, Alice grows in every which way, but she does not grow up. With a swig of "DRINK ME" potion, she "shuts up like a telescope," wondering if she "might go out altogether, like a candle." But as soon as she swallows a bite of "EAT ME" cake, her neck and limbs elongate as in a funhouse mirror; she says goodbye to her feet. Like Alice, time in Wonderland dilates, contracts, stops. The Mad Hatter's handless watch stands perpetually at tea time, two days late. Time, he explains to Alice, has quarreled with the Queen and refuses to budge. Instead, the guests rotate around the tea table in an endless loop. Time in Wonderland is the time of dreams, or childhood. It's unruly, disobedient, both slippery and stuck.

Published in 1865, *Alice in Wonderland* is often seen as Lewis Carroll's response to the increasingly regulated industrial society of mid-Victorian England. The book came out less than two decades after the British Railway Clearing House synchronized its schedules to the prime meridian in Greenwich, and just six years after the Great Clock at Westminster Palace first chimed the nation's hours. Factory workers and school children alike now obeyed Big Ben instead of nature. For the first time in human history, time was decoupled from the diurnal movement of the sun.

Control of time, of course, is power. In 1906, Bombay factory workers rioted in the streets to protest the switch to Indian Standard Time, which they saw (rightly) as an imposition of British colonial rule. Nepal held out, setting its

128

clocks to the Gauri Shankar Meridian instead of Greenwich. As a result, Nepal Standard Time is five hours and forty-five minutes ahead of England, and fifteen minutes ahead of India (hence the joke that Nepalis are always fifteen minutes late). In the United States, 144 different time zones coexisted until the standardization of "railway time" in 1883; Congress did not pass the Standard Time Act, legally codifying the five time zones, until 1918. Even today, Arizona refuses to "spring forward" to daylight saving time, as do Puerto Rico, Hawaii, the U.S. Virgin Islands, American Samoa, and Guam.

∞

Time, in my family, was a kind of craziness—what Yiddish speakers call a *mishegas*. My grandfather, regimented as the Austro-Hungarian officer he once was, ran a textile factory, and my father was an industrial engineer. The *tick-tick-tick* of manufacturing efficiency tapped out the rhythm of their lives. You had to be *pünktlich*—or else. There was no tolerance for deviation from the plan, even when it didn't matter in the least. Show up late for lunch? *Unforgivable!* Head to the beach a bit later than planned? *Impossible!* Flexible and spontaneous we were not.

My father was reliably early for every get-together, doctor's appointment, meeting, restaurant reservation, even the most informal date. He never got to the airport less than three hours before a flight, much to my mother's irritation. If you weren't ready when he was—which is to say, at least fifteen minutes before whatever time he'd planned to meet— he'd swear and badger, fume and pace. He far preferred to wait around, bored, than deal with the intolerable anxiety that he might be late.

In my worst dreams, an exam is about to start for a course I'd forgotten I was taking, or my plane is about to board and I'm still at home and haven't even begun to pack.

I'm paralyzed, fixed in place. I'm staring at the pile of unread books, at the suitcase lying empty on the bed. The White Rabbit's cry is clanging in my ears: *late, late, late, late.*

∞

Unsurprisingly, my father loved watches. He liked to window-shop at the jewelry stores along Madison Avenue in New York and the Bahnhofstrasse in Zurich, pointing out the brands he deemed the best. We peered together through the shop windows at the watches that stood like little busts in a museum on their angled velvet stands. I memorized their names: Omega, Longines, Movado, Breitling, Patek Philippe. The watches had bejeweled bezels, gold or platinum bracelets, faces adorned with suns and moons and dials, delicately ticking hands.

My father did not own a fancy watch. A technologist at heart, he was partial to lightweight, inexpensive timepieces. Above all, he was interested in the watch industry's story of disruptive innovation. Wristwatch sales had boomed after World War I, making pocket watches obsolete. The bulletproof-glass faces, turntable bezels, and glow-in-the-dark dials designed for soldiers transformed the dainty lady's accessory into a manly, utilitarian tool. Innovation followed. In 1926, Rolex introduced the first waterproof case, followed by the self-winding mechanism in 1931, and the automatic date window in 1945. Swiss watchmakers quickly came to dominate the market; "Swiss watch" became synonymous with reliability and precision. James Bond sported an Omega, as did astronaut Jim Lovell, who used his NASA-issued Omega Speedmaster to time the mission-saving fuel burn on Apollo 13.

In the 1970s, everything abruptly changed. Capitalizing on quartz technology (an American invention), Japanese manufacturers flooded the market with cheap, electronic timepieces. Casio, Citizen, and Orient soon topped global sales, and Swiss watch exports dropped by sixty percent in less than ten years. Still, the Swiss fought back with innovative designs and marketing. By 1993 Swatch had become the best-selling watch in the history of the industry. My father was impressed by Seiko, thrilled by Swatch.

I have saved my grandfather's pocket watch, my father's Breitling, my grandmother's gold wristwatch with its slender band. I still have the little Timex my father gave me for my seventh birthday, the square-faced Omega he bought me when I graduated from high school, the Movado he gave me when I started my first job, the stainless-steel Tissot he got me when I turned fifty. None of them still ticks. These days I wear an Apple watch instead.

The watch my father wore until he died, a solar-powered titanium Pulsar, sits on my desk, soaking up the light. It will run forever, my father always said. So far, he is right.

∞

For years, I tried to keep track of time in notebooks. In a plastic bin at the back of my closet, I've saved my old journals, assignment books from high school, leather-bound date diaries from work. Every once in a while I pull one out and flip through the pages. Why do I remember some things but not others? Often I'm as struck by what's *not* there as by what I do remember. (The day I met my husband? The day my first book was published? Not a trace.) Now I keep a dry-erase calendar on my fridge; each month I wipe it clean and start again. I keep track of my appointments online on Google Calendar, synced to my watch, which helpfully tap-taps my wrist ten minutes in advance to make sure I'm never late.

I first kept a diary in the summer after fourth grade when I was nine. The wide-ruled pages of the little paperback,

filled with my wobbly script, are mostly a ship's log of my
family's emotional weather. Were my parents getting along or
fighting? Was my brother being good or bratty? Was I feeling
bored or angry, excited or misunderstood? Here and there, I
decorated the pages with stickers and little drawings. In the
centerfold, I taped a postcard from the Okefenokee Swamp
in Georgia, sent to me by a boy in my class named Edmund
G. On the back, in cramped grade-school cursive, he has
written only this: *I love you! I love you! I love you! I love you!* I
don't remember much liking Edmund, who got scolded by
the teacher for writing with sooty pencil stubs and drawing
swastikas on his desk. I'm pretty sure I never talked to him
again. Yet even after all these years, his words give me the
same faint twinge of embarrassment and pleasure and anxiety
each time I see them. And then I shut the diary, and the
moment tucks itself away again between the pages of
the book.

∞

I am seven or eight. I'm hanging around my
grandfather's bedroom as he gets ready to go out. He buttons
his shirt, ties his shoes. He lays his wristwatch across his palm
and holds it out. It has a plain round face, a sturdy leather
strap. The watch is solid and serious, like him.

"You must turn the hands like so," he says, pulling out
the stem, showing me how to adjust the time. "*Never* the
other way."

He gives me a stern look, as if he's showing me how to
tune a Stradivarius or defuse a bomb. He pushes the stem in
and rubs the crown between his thick forefinger and thumb.

"You must always wind the watch at the same time,
every day," he says. "You must not forget. *Verstehst-du?*"

I nod obediently. He hands me his watch, and I hold
it to my ear.

The tiny wheels and gears have all been set in motion. The mechanism whirrs and swishes, like a secret heart.

∞

Nostalgia, like hoarfrost, forms under particular atmospheric conditions. In my parents' house, it seems, the climate is exactly right. Because they stayed put for so many years, and because my own apartments and houses have had so little storage space, I never properly moved out. My mother sleeps in "my" room now, and even though her toiletries line the bathroom shelves, and her clothes fill the dresser drawers, and the scent of her perfume hangs in the air, my old barrettes and books and knickknacks are still there as well, as if someday I might be coming back.

My mother, a child of the Great Depression, can't bear to throw things out. Every object in the house is imbued with value, which is to say with memory and significance—even the junk. I poke around the cabinets in my old room and find a tin of crumbling sand dollars I collected as a kid, a golden mask I once brought back from Venice, shoeboxes full of letters and postcards from my grandparents and friends. In the nightstand, I find a time-capsule cigar box filled with random memorabilia: a child's ski lift pass from Sun Valley, a ticket to the 1976 Harvard-Yale game, a *Peanuts* cartoon, the hospital wristband from when I got my wisdom teeth out, the arm of a long-lost ceramic doll.

My mother brings out a pile of sweaters that have been there since I left for college and lays them on the bed. There's a nubby blue-green cardigan she knit for me in middle school, two Fair Isle sweaters we picked out together at the Burlington Arcade in London, an Austrian jacket made of light-blue boiled wool. A rime of nostalgia clings to every fiber, even though I haven't worn these sweaters in more than forty years, even though there's no way they still fit.

"Nobody makes nice things like this anymore," my mother says.

I say, "Mom, you can't downsize one sweater at a time."

We decide to send the sweaters to my daughter. Everything else stays where it is.

∞

The word "nostalgia" was coined in 1688 by a Swiss medical student, Johannes Hofer, to describe a strange wasting disease observed in young people living abroad. Hofer's neologism combined the Greek words *nosos* ("return to one's native land") and *algos* ("suffering and grief"). The symptoms included anxiety, nausea, anorexia, sleep disturbances, obsessive thoughts, heart palpitations, thirst, weakness, sluggishness, hopelessness, fevers, even death. Nostalgia, Hofer theorized, was a neurological ailment brought on by an "afflicted imagination." Obsessive memories of home caused the "vital spirits" to flow into the brain, depriving bodily systems of the "essential ethers" needed for good health. Fortunately, there was a cure. The patient only needed to go home again.

Homelessness lies at the hollow core of Jewish history. As a people, we've been sent into exile again and again since the first Assyrian expulsion from Samaria in the eighth century BCE. Over the centuries, the Jews were expelled from Rome, Judea, England, Spain, Portugal, Hungary, Yemen, Germany. My father lost his childhood home when his family fled Nazi-occupied Czechoslovakia for Palestine in 1940, when he was not yet ten. He came to the United States in 1952, at twenty-two, alone. He met my mother two years later, and they settled down in the house they bought to fill the empty space left by the violent upheavals of the past. My father could not return to Czechoslovakia; my mother could not return to Lithuania; they did not want to live in Israel.

If my father felt nostalgic for the place he was born—for the country where his ancestors had lived for more than twenty generations—he never spoke about it. There could be no going back.

Today, neither "nostalgia" nor "homesickness" is specified as a diagnosis in the American Psychiatric Association's *Diagnostic and Statistical Manual of Mental Disorders* (DSM). "Homesickness," in its most extreme forms, is now considered a type of "separation anxiety disorder" (F93.0), an "adjustment disorder with mixed anxiety and depressed mood" (F43.23), or an "acculturation difficulty, cultural maladjustment or shock" (V60.3). Nostalgia, on the other hand, is merely a "sentimental longing for or regretful memory of a period of the past" (*Oxford English Dictionary*), less a malady than a self-indulgence, a yearning tied to time and memory, not place.

I've lived in Cambridge, Oxford, London, New York, Salt Lake City, and Ohio since I left home for college. I've had at least a dozen different home addresses. Now I have a big house of my own filled with my young-adult children's childhood belongings that I don't know what to do with. Should we save the LEGOs and the PLAYMOBIL? The wooden trains or books or blocks or dolls? I have no regrets, of course, that my kids have launched into their independent lives, but I can't shake my sentimental longing for the past. I steel myself against it, but the ache persists.

∞

In his 1992 *New Yorker* essay, "Out of Kansas," Salman Rushdie wonders why Dorothy is so keen to get back home from Oz. "The Kansas described by Frank Baum is a depressing place," Rushdie writes. "Everything in it is gray as far as the eye can see." Filmed in black and white on an MGM soundstage, Hollywood's Kansas is a bleak, hardscrabble expanse of meanness and poverty that anybody would yearn to escape. Oz, on the other hand, is a Technicolor paradise. There, Dorothy is no troublemaker, but intelligent and kind and brave. And yet the Yellow Brick Road leads back to Kansas. "There's no place like home," Glinda intones, and Dorothy repeats, clicking her ruby heels. Rushdie doesn't buy it. He writes:

> The truth is that, once we leave our childhood places and start to make up our lives, armed only with what we know and who we are, we come to understand that the real secret of the ruby slippers is not that 'there's no place like home' but, rather, that there is no longer any such place as home—except, of course, for the homes we make, or the homes that are made for us, in Oz. Which is anywhere—and everywhere—except the place from which we began.

Not being able to go home again is the plight of the immigrant, like my father, or the writer-in-exile, like Rushdie. The wish for home is no passing dream, but a longing for a place that exists only in the imagination, forever beyond reach.

∞

My father was pretty lucky in the end, though not quite as lucky as his own father, who at ninety-seven felt unwell one day and was gone the next. Up to his early nineties, my father suffered from relatively minor ailments: glaucoma, gout, A-fib, neuropathy on the bottoms of his feet. But gradually— so slowly, in fact, that we scarcely noticed it—he started slowing down. He complained of "weakness" and dizziness, had trouble sleeping. He started walking with a shuffle, leaning on a cane. He spent more and more time sitting at his desk in silence, staring into space. His handwriting grew shaky. He lost his appetite, lost weight. Still, we told ourselves he had a few more good years in him. His memory and awareness were still sharp, his wits still keen.

Then the hospital stays began. Doctors scrambled to regulate his plummeting body temperature, his kidney function, his white blood cell count, his blood pressure, the accumulated fluid pressing on his heart. Every time he was admitted, he fell into a hospital-induced delirium. He slept through visiting hours, stayed awake all night. He grew agitated and disoriented. He tried to pull the IVs out of his arm, lashed out at the nurses, and demanded to be released. At other times, he'd fall into a deep somnolence, unable to open his eyes or speak or eat. He was still alive, but he wasn't really there.

"If you can't eat, you can't live," the doctor said gently. My mother and brother and I opted against a feeding tube. Day after day, we sat by my father's side. There was nothing to be done but wait.

Two months before he passed away, we moved him to a hospice facility near his home. For a full day after the transfer, he did not wake up. My mother begged the staff to dial back the sedatives. The next day, he opened his eyes and began to speak. He seemed to be inside a waking dream. He urged me to contact the governors of Massachusetts, New Hampshire, and Rhode Island to warn them to stockpile water in advance of an invasion. He ordered me to book him a flight to Orly Airport in Paris, where he said he had a meeting with General de Gaulle. He began to dictate a detailed consulting report on the global semiconductor industry. "Did you see what I wrote for CNN?" he whispered, then confided, "We have many enemies." Like any dream, it made no sense, and yet it did.

On the third day after the transfer, I arrived at the hospice to find him sitting up in bed, his eyes sharp and focused, his mind completely clear. It was like looking at the sky after a storm. "Good morning, darling," he said. "Where am I?" I handed him a calendar, and he stared at it,

137

counting and recounting the weeks since he'd gone into the hospital two months earlier, shaking his head. He'd left home in January; now it was nearly March. He'd lost more than forty pounds. He was so weak he couldn't feed himself, sit up unassisted, much less get out of bed.

Against the odds, he started to recover. He began to eat. He asked for his cell phone. He put on his watch. He demanded physical therapy. He begged his dentist to come and refit his dentures. Before long, he was able to stand up. Soon he was trotting up and down the hall, pushing his walker, his johnny flapping open at the back. "Everybody in this goddamn place is practically dead except for me!" he joked. The hospice nurses laughed and shook their heads.

More than anything, he wanted to go home. He wanted to sit in his office, see his paintings, look out at his yard. He begged my brother to drive him over to the house, just for a visit. I didn't think the hospice staff would allow it, but they did. I thought of Ellen Langer's "Counterclockwise" subjects in their farmhouse time warp. Maybe going home would help my father, too. My brother texted me a photo of him standing at his desk, sorting through the accumulated stacks of bills and mail. He looked very thin, but very much himself, with his bald head and reading glasses, a gray knit shirt tucked into navy pants. I posted the photo on Facebook. "I'm happy to say that he's recovering!" I wrote, and 215 friends clicked "like."

But I was wrong. Within nine days, he was back in the ICU. An infection had started raging, undetected, and he was in septic shock. Two weeks later, he was gone.

∞

It is said that the trick of memorization known as the "memory palace" was first used by the sixth century Greek poet Simonides of Ceos after a banquet hall collapsed, killing everyone inside. Simonides, who had stepped out of the hall just before the disaster and found himself the sole survivor, was able to identify the bodies by remembering the specific places they'd been sitting before disaster struck. This coupling of memory with place, neuroscientists have since discovered, is encoded in the fundamental structures of the brain. "Time cells" in the hippocampus switch on as events unfold, keeping a record of the flow of time, while "place cells" activate as we pass through specific locations. "Grid cells" in the entorhinal cortex encode the sequence of events in both time and space.

In the days after my father's death, I walk around my parents' house, taking pictures on my phone. I take pictures of the kitchen, the living room, the dining room, his office, the paintings, the yard and pool and pond. I take a picture of the stairs, whose creaking music still sounds the way it did each morning when my dad went down to breakfast. I take pictures of the drawers of his desk, still filled with his notebooks and pens and little tins of mints; of the ancient Roman glass bottles, lit by sunlight, hanging in the window; of the telephone handset that still smells like pipe tobacco, even though it has been nearly forty years since he last smoked. Will these images help me remember? Looking at them now, they all feel flat. What will I be able to hold onto once everything is gone?

∞

In the final days after my father was discharged from the ICU and sent back to hospice, we struggled to face our feelings. Sitting by his bed, my brother and I scrolled on our phones. Our mother read. We didn't talk or weep. The nursing staff came in and out. Once, there came a knock at the door, and a cantor from a local synagogue peeked in. He asked if he could help. My parents sent him away. I wanted to object, but I did not.

I don't want to remember those last few days and hours.

The pain that could not be touched by morphine. The way his features sank. The gurgling breath. If I could turn time back, I wouldn't leave his room that final night when it grew late. I would stay until the very end. I would hold his hand.

My father didn't want a funeral. He wanted to be cremated. He wanted his remains to be scattered in the mountains, beneath the cold, bright sky and snowy peaks, among aspens, spruce and pines. I wanted to honor his wishes, of course, but I didn't like the idea of smoke and ashes. I longed for the comfort of timeworn words and ritual, not silence. I wanted a place where I could leave a pebble. I wanted his memory to be a blessing. I wanted to hold on.

In the Jewish tradition, sacred texts—Torah scrolls, the Talmud, even a scrap printed with the words of the Hebrew bible—are never thrown away. They're stored instead inside a genizah, a special area (usually in the attic or cellar of a synagogue) until they can be given a proper burial, like any other once-living thing.

My parents' house is a genizah, I think. If only, when the time comes, we could dig a hole and bury the house and all its contents in it. I would kneel and bend my head in prayer. I'd say kaddish for the dead.

AUTHOR'S NOTE

This collection has been many years in the making. "Secret Agent Man" was first published in 2005, "Counterclockwise" in 2025. I didn't set out to write a book about my father, or even a collection. The essays have come together around the themes of time and history, obscurity and clarity, memory and forgetting. As the essays have accumulated, of course, the world has turned and changed. In some cases, I have made revisions to bring certain details up to date. In other cases, I have left them be.

I am grateful to the following literary journals for publishing many of the essays in this collection (at times in somewhat different form): *Third Coast,* "Secret Agent Man"; *Defunct,* "The Power Suit"; *Conjunctions* (web edition), "Ghost Variations"; *The Sun,* "The Brahmic Egg"; *The Normal School,* "Call It Rape"; *Ninth Letter,* "A Natural History of Small-Town Ohio"; *River Teeth,* "Afterimage" and "Counterclockwise."

Many thanks go as well to Jessica Hendry Nelson and Sean Prentiss for including "Call It Rape" in *Advanced Creative Nonfiction* (Bloomsbury Academic, 2020); to Steven Church for selecting it for *The Spirit of Disruption* (Outpost19, 2018); and to the editors of *Longreads* for syndicating it as a Member Exclusive in December 2012. Thanks to Jocelyn Morin for reprinting "Ghost Variations" in *Above Ground* (Harvard Square Editions, 2009). I am also grateful to the editors of Houghton-Mifflin's *Best American Essays* anthology series for designating as Notable Essays "Afterimage" (in 2019) and "A Natural History of Small-Town Ohio" (in 2011).

Heartfelt thanks are due to Pam Balluck, Peter Covino, Charles Kell, Rachel Rothenberg, and the rest of the wonderful team at Barrow Street for pulling this manuscript out of the contest pile, and for all your wise guidance and staunch support along the way. A special nod is due to Robin Hemley, in whose graduate workshop I first drafted "Secret Agent Man" and "The Brahmic Egg," launching me on my way. Denison University's R. C. Good and Bowen sabbatical fellowships gave me much-needed time to write. Residencies at UCross, Yaddo, and Ragdale provided quiet space, good food, and inspiring company. I am deeply grateful for the feedback, encouragement, and support from Michael Croley, Melissa Faliveno, Peter Grandbois, Jennifer Leonard, David McGlynn, Cass McNally, Jessica Hendry Nelson, Dennis Read, Jack Shuler, Ann Townsend, Nicole Walker, and many others.

This is a work of nonfiction. I have tried to be as truthful as it is humanly possible to be. I've researched and checked my facts. To my family and friends, thank you for your equanimity. Any errors or misrepresentations are mine alone.

MARGOT SINGER is the author of a novel, *Underground Fugue*, and a linked short story collection, *The Pale of Settlement*. She is also the co-editor, with Nicole Walker, of *Bending Genre: Essays on Creative Nonfiction*. She is the recipient of the Flannery O'Connor Award, the Edward Lewis Wallant Award, the Reform Judaism Prize, the Glasgow Prize, the James Jones First Novel Fellowship, as well as grants from the NEA and the Ohio Arts Council. A professor of creative writing at Denison University, she lives with her family in Granville, Ohio.

BARROW STREET PRESS - recent titles:

Zounds! Aleksander Zywicki 2025
Unlikely Skylight, Hollis Kurman 2025
Secret Agent Man, Margot Singer 2025
An Anthology of Rain, Phillis Levin 2025
Spare, Michelle Lewis 2025
The Mouth Is Also a Compass, Carrie Bennett 2024
Brutal Companion, Ruben Quesada 2024
Brother Nervosa, Ronald Palmer 2024
The Fire Road, Nicholas Yingling 2024
Close Red Water, Emma Aylor 2023
Fanling in October, Pui Ying Wong 2023
Landscape with Missing River, Joni Wallace 2023
Down Low and Lowdown..., Timothy Liu 2023
the archive is all in present tense, Elizabeth Hoover 2022
Person, Perceived Girl, A.A. Vincent 2022
Frank Dark, Stephen Massimilla 2022
Liar, Jessica Cuello 2021
On the Verge of Something Bright and Good, Derek Pollard 2021
The Little Book of No Consolation, Becka Mara McKay 2021
Shoreditch, Miguel Murphy 2021
Hey Y'all Watch This, Chris Hayes 2020
Uses of My Body, Simone Savannah 2020
Vortex Street, Page Hill Starzinger 2020
Exorcism Lessons in the Heartland, Cara Dees 2019
American Selfie, Curtis Bauer 2019
Hold Sway, Sally Ball 2019
Green Target, Tina Barr 2018
Luminous Debris: New & Selected Legerdemain, Timothy Liu 2018
We Step into the Sea: New and Selected Poems, Claudia Keelan 2018
Adorable Airport, Jacqueline Lyons 2018
Whiskey, X-ray, Yankee, Dara-Lyn Shrager 2018

For a complete list of publications go to: https://barrowstreet.org